Sleight of Hand – *"An Entrepreneur's Bag of Tricks"* will challenge how you define an entrepreneur or business leader. Not everyone was meant to be an entrepreneur and no matter what role you play in life, it is up to you to decide if you want to be the magician or the audience. Are you ready to see behind the curtain? Enclosed are the tricks and tools you need to be an entrepreneur. Whether a master magician or a budding entrepreneur, this book will motivate or Dmotivate you to pursue the journey of building something successful.

SLEIGHT OF HAND

An Entrepreneur's Bag of Tricks

DRU T. RIESS II

Clovercroft Publishing

Sleight of Hand

Published by Clovercroft Publishing, Franklin, Tennessee

Senior Editor: Tammy Kling

Executive Editor: Tiarra Tompkins

Copy Editor: Christy Callahan

Cover Design by Sarah Thurstenson

Interior Design by Suzanne Lawing

Printed in the United States of America

978-1-948484-61-9

Sleight of hand is also known as *prestidigitation* or *legerdemain* and refers to *fine motor skills* when used by performing artists in different art forms to entertain or manipulate. It is closely associated with *close-up magic, card cheating, card flourishing,* and in my opinion all BUSINESS. The life of an entrepreneur or business leader involves persistence, creativity, smoke, mirrors, acumen, and a sleight of hand.

Contents

Introduction

Have you ever heard people associate life with one big rat race?

Sayings like that make you wonder: Who are we racing against? Is it really a race? Is it a show? At times it feels like there is an audience watching us all scramble to climb and reach higher heights. If it is a race, then our parents and ancestors must have run qualifying heats, and now we are forced to settle for where they ended their journey. Whether rich or poor, you are born into the starting blocks of your race or born into your part of the performance. If your parents were rich, you might be too. If they were poor, that's your fate. Is that fair? Of course not.

Lesson #1: Life isn't fair.

The silver spoon kids get lane 1 on the inside of the track, and the others get lanes 7 or 8, and some of us don't even get a ticket inside the stadium.

Have you ever thought about it like that?

The truth about the world is, it's not only a race against time; it's merely one grand illusion. You are raised with imaginary bumpers to make you conform to what is socially acceptable and make you think that there is nothing possible to obtain outside the lane of your circumstances. There are greater powers at work here that do not want to see people succeed, there are government regulations that continue to suppress those trying to come up, and it's going to be an uphill battle if you ever want to get out of the faction you were born into. Unless you use a Sleight of Hand and don't allow them to see you coming up!

Why is it that when you get a bonus at work it is taxed at a higher rate than your regular income? Government regulations make sure you don't get too far ahead! Why, when you die, is the inheritance that you leave to your loved ones taxed again? I don't care if there's a $5 million gifting allowance before taxation hits; it's still not fair to be double taxed. How much sense does that make? Isn't that double taxation? You already paid taxes on that money when you worked hard and earned it. Why should the government get to double dip into the inheritance that is meant for the ones you love? During a time of grieving, your family members find themselves dividing your assets and worrying about what they owe personally now for being gifted anything of value. Once again, government regulation is trying to make sure you don't leave your faction!

Just like the characters in the movies *The Hunger Games* or *Divergent*, you may be born into one faction or another and limited by whom you are surrounded with. Are you rich, or are you poor? Are you nobility or a peasant? Much of your destiny is determined by where or how you grew up, and this simple truth has existed from the beginning of time.

In the movie *In Time*, the wealthy have longer lives. Time is currency. The underlying message in these kinds of movies is suppression and systems where the rich stay rich and the poor stay poor. Sure, the rich are willing to sell you their secrets, *but only at their gain*. None of these people care or want to see you rise up. This is not just a Hollywood movie, but a reality of the world we live in. Anyone selling you something or giving you something is doing it for their gain. None of these people are telling you the truth about business. These people just want to sell you false hope. Don't buy into it!

In fact, it's likely that even the motivational speakers, authors, or life coaches you're listening to have been led down the path of motivational nonsense. Go ahead, look up the author's background to discover what they have achieved in their professional career. I have a friend who is brainwashed by John Maxwell and his leadership techniques, but when I researched Maxwell, I learned that he was a pastor who then turned into a motivational speaker/author. Think about that. Your original blueprint is the Bible, but then you decide to write books that are a small departure from the Bible.

All pastors are good at twisting words to make a story relative for that particular audience. Even the ones with the kindest, purest hearts are aware of how to present their words to an audience. All pastors are selling their message and performing the act that keeps their audience engaged. Pastors teach from the Bible (there is only one Bible) and all of them try to make the delivery of their messages original. All successful pastors get people to follow them, but being a pastor comes with the mother of all blueprints (the Bible).

Some pastors do it better than others and some not so much. Some pastors are genuine and others have selfish motives. If you need spiritual motivation, if you want hope, if you're looking for words, then dive into a John Maxwell book; but if you're a businessman or woman, why would you follow a man who was not made building a business? Why would you ask your team at work to follow a man who knows nothing about business? If you want results, why are you looking for *words*? Why follow a guy who has never done something original?

Entrepreneurship is the epitome of being original. Yes, John's leadership analogies are convincing and relatable, but they were not his experiences and they're mostly just *words*.

Furthermore, any motivational speaker would have nothing if it weren't for clueless individuals who want answers but are looking in all the wrong places. Shame on these people for preying on the weak!

When any motivational author writes of leadership, they are theorists and philosophers. Most authors are not taught by firsthand trial and error. There are exceptions to the rule, however, such as Nick Vujicic, who speaks from true life experiences and struggles of being born with no arms and legs. NOW THAT IS SOMEONE TO LISTEN TO ABOUT OVERCOMING ADVERSITY, DEPRESSION, AND CHANNELING INNER DRIVE.

Look up Tony Robbins' credentials! Did you know he started his first job at seventeen as a promoter for another motivational speaker's seminar? No business experience! None! Did you know that motivational speaker was Jim Rohn? From there, he continued in the brainwashed industry of motivational speaking and has basically regurgitated the same information for decades, but none of the information was original. No real-life struggles of his own. No trauma that was real. Nothing but Hollywood smoke and mirrors. Tony had blueprints from Jim Rohn. Tony had people invested in him to sell himself and prey on helpless people looking for hope and *words*. Tony sought out how to hypnotize people and learned how to walk across fire rocks—"true story." These two tricks were all it took for him to build a brand out of a house of cards copying those he followed, like Jim Rohn. Tony and his corruption built a brand that is all smoke and mirrors, and now they even sell you nutritional supplements that are probably laced with something to keep you addicted to his hypnosis. You think those products are of good quality or are intended to help you? Think again! It's all for Tony's gain and none of his followers. What business owner or entrepreneur has a blueprint for building their business? There is none! **Building a business, being a leader, and being an entrepreneur is all about instincts.**

There is no blueprint. Sure, Tony has owned businesses now, but *he has never been the entrepreneur in the sense you could or would relate to.* So why would you read a book of his and believe you can make it in business? He's never been the guy back against the wall leading a group of people from the first brick to the last. It's the Tony Show! He's a grandiose, sole proprietor in business terms if you ask me.

When it comes to marriage, relationships, kids, family, and day-to-day life, I absolutely promote self-help books, motivational speakers, and others who temporarily inspire. The goal in these situations is to find the best "you"—and most of the time the "you" that others can coexist with. But this book is about entrepreneurship. This book is about figuring out whether you have it or not.

In entrepreneurship there is no place for motivational speakers!

In entrepreneurship there is no place for motivational speakers!

In entrepreneurship there is no place for motivational speakers!

Being an entrepreneur is a natural ability. There is no teaching and no learning that can make you an entrepreneur or not. It's in your DNA or it isn't.

To teach someone something means they grasp a concept completely and can repeat a task or regurgitate information they did not know prior to being taught. Yes, you can temporarily inspire someone by giving them a pep talk, but in no way, shape, or form can you be in someone's face 24 hours a day to continue motivating them. It is human nature that stimulants suppress themselves after time. The motivation wears off. People eventually revert back to their natural personalities and natural tendencies, and that's what makes you, you. You can ignite their internal spark, but they have to tend the fire.

You can give examples of how to be a leader, but you can or cannot lead. All the self-help lessons in the world will not make someone who is not wired to be a leader a leader. It's something you are gifted with, and you either have it or you don't, along with the gift of limitations. Some are meant to lead a family and others are meant to lead an army. Not everyone is capable of leading, even when put in the position to lead the smallest number of followers.

Again, this is not a self-help book. This is not a motivational book. I will be aggressive against motivational speakers and their tactics, but please take it in context. The audience reading this book should be entrepreneurs, future entrepreneurs, those questioning their path, and future business grads. I want you to understand how business works, and I'm certainly not here to give you **words**!

I decided to chronicle the journey of my growth as an entrepreneur after I'd experienced a lot of struggles and victories along the way. Success is sugarcoated in society today. Everyone who achieves success wants you to believe that it came to them effortlessly, but I am the voice of truth. Success is hard as f--- to make happen, and you will cry—damn, you will cry—on your journey! A lot of the time I had no idea what I was doing, but I kept on going, kept on selling, and continued working hard when my back was against the wall. I often felt like a magician, and what I realized was I was blazing the trail for my industry to follow. Thus, I was creating the blueprint. I did it all while slipping through the social barriers and climbing to a place in this world I was never supposed to be able to get to. I beat the system!

This book is a tool for you to use at every point in your journey.

At the end of this book, I have placed blank pages for you to take notes. This is just my story—not a Bible of business or life. Use the blank pages to begin your legacy, record your story, refute my views, or write questions you would ask me or some other business leader if given the opportunity to in person.

1

♠

Are You a Magician?

What if I told you there are strategies you can use while building a business that are characteristic of a master magician? What if how I escaped my faction is something that is coachable? Is that a new way for you to look at business?

What if I could teach you how to distract your competition while you breach the gates with a Trojan Horse? What if I could teach you how to blur your audience's vision while slipping out the trap door?

It's all a matter of magic. From shell games to Sleight of Hand, from smoke and mirrors to suspenseful endings. Call it marketing, and I'll call it tricking your customer. Call it sales if you want, but I call it performing an act. Defend how it's ethical, and I'll expose it for what it really is. That's business.

Business requires an element of magic. Some call it luck, but there is no such thing as luck. If you work hard and you play your cards right, anything is possible. Sounds like magic to me!

My goal with this book is to educate those in business or those going into business about what is real and what is illusion. Let's call it what it is. You can't make someone lead who wasn't born to lead, and you can't motivate people who don't have an element of autonomy. Most motivational speakers and authors are not changing you; rather, they are showing you how to "act" like a leader. They are teaching you how to "act" motivating. I'm telling you, it is a show, and if you agree with this very basic principle, then there is hope for you. I'm telling you the whole world is an illusion. How can you trick people to get what you want in life? How can you "act" like someone others will follow, buy from, get motivated by, or learn from? Take it from a guy who truly built a business from ashes and who can write by reflecting on real-life experiences. You can't teach entrepreneurship, and you can't teach leadership. You either have "IT" or you don't.

Have you ever heard about the "IT" factor? This is where that applies.

If you don't have the "IT" factor, then you reach for these motivational books/leadership books to help you learn how to perform as someone who has the "IT" factor. Most of the time those trying to teach it don't even possess it themselves. In no way are those books capable of changing who you are, but if you realize what they are doing, perhaps they will be more effective. It's not about changing you; it's about getting you to "act" like something you're not naturally. This book is intended to help you vet yourself. Do you have the "IT" factor, or are you one looking to simply mimic those that do to get ahead in life? My goal at the end of the book is that you at least know which one you are and whether or not you have what it takes to elevate out of what you were born into.

Are you just a performer putting on an act? Are you a master magician? Or, can you at least act as someone worth watching?

One of my pet peeves is watching motivational speakers talk to a room of people and tell them that they can *all* do it!

But they can't. Not everyone is created equal in all things. We are not born cookie cutter from the same mold in this world. Every single person will have his or her individual strengths and weaknesses. Our country has a lot of historical figures who have loosely thrown that verbiage around without truly assessing what that would mean to society. No one is created equal! Not everyone wins a trophy either!

I'm so tired of watching people spend money and mortgaging their house on things they just aren't cut out to do. One of the reasons for my parents' divorce was over debt, and particularly credit card debt, so this is personal for me. I am sure to be a dissenting and controversial voice in the motivational speaking world, but that's not my mission here. If anything, I'm here to **demotivate** you from making irrational decisions. (Note: my first name is Dru, and thus I will use the first letter of my name and attach it to 'motivation' for my coined spelling of the term dmotivation). My mission is to help you be your authentic self and from there know when you're not being your true self. My mission is to expose where you may be a victim to a Sleight of Hand and how to see the Sleight of Hand around you.

At times not being "you" will be intentional to close a deal, to get someone to do something you want them to do, or to fit into or retain a particular audience. At times and possibly most of the time, people won't want your authentic self. Entrepreneurs are magicians, and your lack of authenticity becomes a part of the "act." Be able to see the illusion for what it is and appreciate the magician behind it.

My motivation for writing this book is to expose the truth. I love reality shows like *Shark Tank* as much as the next person. I love watching what unique ideas or products people invent, and I like learning different ways to form a deal. What I don't like is that a lot of the times the deals they do make inflate the success those businesses have. It is anything but reality, and it gives entrepreneurs a false sense of success and a misrepresentation of what it means to be an entrepreneur.

At times they make it sound like millions of dollars in sales means being that huge success that everyone is looking for. In one example, they bragged how since *Shark Tank* aired a year ago, they now have $1.5 million in sales. I watch that, knowing the illusion, and I'm furious. To have $1.5 million in sales is nothing, but the general public hears the word *million* and associates these small entrepreneurs to being millionaires now. I repeat, to sell $1.5 million of anything is equivalent to a child selling 20 glasses of lemonade at the end of their driveway! This is lying by "selective word choice." In reality, if you know how it works, they might have a 25–35 percent gross margin on that $1.5 million in sales, but then they have everyday expenses to run the business such as salaries, office supplies, legal fees, accounting fees, HR fees, healthcare (if you offer it and if you don't, then that shows just how small of a company you are), other benefits, taxes, rent or mortgage payment for your place of business, travel and entertainment, marketing, advertising, and more. When selling lemonade at the end of your driveway, no one gets a salary, your parents paid for the lemonade and other ingredients, and you have no other overhead! After all of this, you might net 15 percent EBITDA (which is what your company is valued on).[1]

---

[1] EBITDA is a measure of a company's ability to produce *income* on its operations in a given year. It is calculated as the company's *revenue* less most of its *expenses* (such as *overhead*) but not subtracting its *tax liability*, *interest* paid on *debt*, *amortization* or *depreciation*. It is important to note that EBITDA does not account for one-off or otherwise unusual revenues and expenses, only recurring ones. It is the number that you multiply when selling your business for x times EBITDA. You want to know this number monthly, as this is where you get your company's net worth.

On $1.5 million in sales, a 15 percent EBITDA is $225,000. At the end of the year that $225,000 in EBITDA does not mean you have anywhere close to $225,000 in cash or $225,000 in realized gains; however, for this scenario we will keep the math simple. Cash is king and perhaps in this case you have $150,000 in cash, but then you have choices to make. Depending on whether you are a corporation or an LLC, you will owe taxes on your realized gains. If you are an LLC and do distribute $150,000 to the shareholders (which I highly advise against as things happen and businesses have slow times where you might need that cash) and you own 60 percent of your company, you get a check for $90,000. Of that $90,000 you now pay an estimated 30 percent or more to Uncle Sam. Now you're sitting there after a $1.5 million in revenue year with $60,000 to $70,000 in extra income. So to recap: one successful year in a perfect and profitable world after making a deal on *Shark Tank,* and you are nowhere near being a millionaire; the odds of you repeating that success for a sustainable amount of time is a ticking time bomb working against you. Keep in mind, I did not even dive into depreciation, book value calculations, and more, which could cause you to pay more or less on your realized gains. Oh, and don't forget the debt you have on the company and the responsible decision you have after having a good year to use any real cash toward the debt of the company.

So why does *Shark Tank* fluff up the success of these small businesses?

You guessed it—ratings!

Ratings make an average person think that they too should take huge risks to reap huge rewards. It's not about the entrepreneur; it's about ABC, CNBC, or whatever network is syndicating the show. It's about pulling an audience for their gain and not yours. So continue watching the show, but understand what is real and what is an illusion. Understand the role you play in ABC or CNBC's success because in this case they are the master magicians. If ABC really wanted to be transparent with the public, they would not bolster the sales of the small business, but rather the EBITDA profit margin!

Can you imagine if that same company said a year after doing a deal on *Shark Tank,* "Our company is almost worth five hundred thousand dollars" (of which you do not own all of the company, so you only get a portion of that)? Not as glamorous—is it?—considering EBITDA is a moving number. One year my shares in my own company were worth several million, and eight months later they were worth nothing! Ownership and net worth, when accumulated through a business you are growing, is like having stock in anything. There will be ups and downs, and you have to stomach the low times as well as the high—the end game being to exit at the highest point!

Let's continue.

2

♠

What I Didn't Know and Found Out the Hard Way

Have you heard it's a "dog eat dog" world out there? Well, that is an understatement for sure. If you're in college deciding whether or not you want to major in business, or if you're a first-time entrepreneur, you need to know what you're getting yourself into. No BS. No sales gimmick. If I'm selling you anything, I'm attempting to sell you peace of mind. I want you to turn around and find a different path.

Business is horrible. No one is your friend, and no one can be trusted. No one is appreciative of you even when they compliment you on your good or service. You're only remembered for your most recent success or failure. The higher you climb, the less you are liked. Everyone is in it for themselves, and I want you to finally get the truth about it. I want you to get the truth from someone not trying to sell you a six-month program to success, but someone who has actually walked the walk of being an entrepreneur. I am telling you right now you will most likely not be successful, but what you do with that information is what determines your future.

Let's start by looking at the definition of *business* and categorizing what a business is. Business according to *Merriam-Webster* is "a commercial or mercantile activity engaged in as a means of livelihood." Are pastors making their living doing anything else? How do they pay their personal bills, buy personal goods, etc? Pastors are a part of a business by definition and so are motivational speakers, executives at nonprofits, educational institutions, etc. It's not a bad thing, but understand the people putting in the work and surviving off monetary returns for their work in all these categories are a part of a business. CEOs and business leaders of nonprofits play by the same rules as Fortune 100 companies and sometimes are even more deceiving. Business is also defined as "dealings or transactions especially of an economic nature between two parties for an act of service or hard asset."

I wish business school had been up-front. I wish people would tell the next generation what to expect and warn them if need be. Thousands of years have gone by and hundreds of years for organized universities, but no one has ever actually taught business for what it is. Sure, they teach you the financial side, how to track it, strategy development, and management solutions, but that's like teaching how the motor of a car works without ever teaching you how to drive it. Business school is a business! Modern-day school is a way to take your money, get you to memorize information, and—guess what—make money!

I know universities are nonprofit, but please spare me. Being nonprofit just means you bleed through all the resources you're given/earn and show a balance of zero on your P&L. The P&L is something they taught me in school! The NCAA Tournament alone grosses over a billion dollars per year.

Please tell me how all that money is precisely spent and how they break even every year.

When I majored in business, why wasn't I told I was majoring in the art of lying and deceit? I don't want to lie for a living, but I spent four years at a public university thinking I was being taught a craft, but instead I was being shoveled useless garbage to memorize and tested on my memorization. In fact, that is the biggest flaw in the American education system. We teach how to memorize facts and not how to problem solve real-world situations. When I minored in marketing, why weren't my teachers up-front with it being a degree in psychological redirection with a focus on being a master manipulator? Why wasn't I taught more of what I would actually use in the real world? Why weren't we told how the Psychology 101 class and sociology electives could be our greatest tool when leaving that institution? Understanding others' behaviors and circumstantial behaviors, as well as controlling an external atmosphere, is key to any business success. Why were these just electives? These electives could very well be all you need to know in business. Everything I did in the business world I could have done with an eigth-grade education. Seriously!

"People are not born corrupt, but rather created." When the CFO of Enron graduated college and went to work his first job, do you think he was corrupt? Do you think someone involved in the Enron corruption, Lehman Brothers' corruption, etc. at the age of twenty-two and newly graduated set out to be corrupt? No! College graduates are full of hope and optimism. Only when they learn about what they have signed up for do they become bitter, feel slighted, and think they've been deceived, and people process that differently.

In college I knew a lady who was a VP at Lehman and lived

on the 30th floor of the Gershwin in New York City. I would go party all of New York on her American Express Black Card in my early twenties. I probably went to New York a handful of times to visit and probably spent $10,000 on her company card. She would tell me to not worry about it and I (being a poor college kid) didn't worry about it! Who would have known Lehman was corrupt?

Those who realize it is a show realize they have a choice to either take while the taking is good or go be average. Those who take while the taking is there get the financial short-term success and climb the ladder, and some can do all of this while staying between the ethical and moral lines of life. The Sleight of Hand techniques I used can be used to advance yourself in society and lead others, all while staying between the moral and ethical lines of humanity. For others, they lose a sense of self and cross the line, all while allowing selfish instincts to direct them. Personally, I am not corrupt, but I have had to dance a dance a time or two to get through a situation or stay politically correct with a clique of people.

For the CFO of Enron, how do you think it went down? Do you think he climbed his way to that position, enjoyed great pay, accustomed his family to a certain level of lifestyle, and then one day discovered the corruption? Do you think he was the root of all the corruption and made it possible from the get-go? Maybe. By that time, do you think he realized the type of trouble he would be in if he came clean? Do you think he didn't second-guess his ethics? Perhaps fear of losing security or losing his family (when I believe we would all do anything for our family) when his hands had blood on them made him act out of character? Have you ever done anything out of character due to external conditions?

Did others know what was going on, yes, but this guy more than likely came into it blindly and later found out. In fact, a lot of people who were innocent were found guilty, but were they born that way? No. Did these people play on the playground as kids corrupt? Did they go through business school corrupt? Do you remember anyone you went to business school with who was corrupt during your college courses? No! Imagine your choices at this point. Imagine a world where we knew the possibilities prior to choosing a major. Had that been the case, I would have chosen E-Media or Industrial Design as a major.

Have you ever realized the Bernie Madoffs of the world are always old as hell when they get busted? At what age did the corruption set in? What was it that pushed them over the edge? Have no doubt, something or someone slighted them and screwed them out of a deal, which exponentially enhanced their greed trait. Like any addiction, often the right thing to do is the hardest thing to do. I'm not saying corruption should be accepted; I'm not saying it's 100 percent something you will come across, but I am asking you to look at what happens in business and has always happened.

Let's talk about this as a reality/possibility in business. What do you do if you find yourself in a situation like this? All I'm saying is that I wish someone would have exposed it and showed me case studies about how, why, and how common it is to be stabbed in the back in business. Later in this book, I will tell you my story about being stabbed in the back and nearly losing everything. In business, every company is against one another. Being partners is a play on words; no one actually wants to be your partner. My suppliers weren't even on my side, but I had to learn that. Your customers will use you over and over and over again with no appreciation for you being the backbone to their success. For you, there is no "I didn't know" after reading this book.

A supplier I bought splicing tape from was playing for his team (his company) and he was against me. Even though I'm buying a product from him, he has to make a margin, and even though I can find the same tape a thousand other places, he sold me on believing his was superior and worth his higher cost. How? Manipulation. Why? Because it's what business is. Eat or be eaten.

My hope is that this book sparks a discussion and inspires modern-day educators to teach tactical skill sets needed in real-world business. If you're teaching someone to be a salesman, teach them to bluff; teach them to tell a white lie. If you're teaching someone to market goods and services, teach them how to manipulate and call it what it is. How do you trick someone into needing something they don't need or could get elsewhere?

Getting your MBA should encompass all the master magician tricks in the book that have built the largest and most prestigious corporations. Every huge corporation has a past and likely one that has secrets. Larger companies have more resources and have legal teams who are experts at the "fine print" we see at the bottom of every commercial or transaction receipt. Larger companies have grown through mergers, acquisition, stabbings of the back to original investors, and more. What if I told you the American Dental Association was formed by Procter & Gamble to sell more toothpaste? Was it? Corrupt or smart? Putting a seal of approval on products gives consumers confidence in their purchase; however, far too often we give those seals too much weight in our decisions.

While I was writing this book, I interviewed several publishing companies. The first marketing company I spoke with talked about positioning the book across college campuses, Hudson newsstands, Amazon, and more. The first suggestion they had, since they knew I had money, was for me to purchase the first 3,000 copies of my own book within the first week. Doing this is all that is needed to make it onto *The New York Times* Best Seller list and secure an Amazon Seal of Approval. I thought, *What the f---? Seriously?* This is a Sleight of Hand, and the company is asking the guy who wrote this book if I'm cool with it.

My younger self would have been astonished this was an option, but the "me" today expected nothing less. I later asked several friends who are avid readers how they pick what they read, and a few of them said they follow *The New York Times* Best Seller list. I laughed and begged them to tell me they were kidding, but they were not. I then disclosed what I just learned about how someone makes *The New York Times* Best Seller list. They were astonished, and all the clout they had given to that list dissipated.

Business is one big magic act where business leaders, entre-preneurs, and CEOs create the impossible or the seemingly impossible. During the growth of your business, you will need to know several tricks or Sleight of Hand distractions to keep your audience seeing only what you want them to see. Some people call it "fake it till you make it" and there's a bit of truth to that, even if you're not really "faking" it—you're just work-ing harder than you let people see.

Would it have been fair to the people buying my book with a *New York Times* Best Seller emblem on it, when no one in the world had ever bought it other than me? Remember life is not fair! What price would you pay to have fans? To have cus-tomers? In the beginning, you have to appear to be successful while you're working hard in order to get others to believe in you. Are you really that surprised there was a trick available if I wanted to pull it out of my hat and sell millions of copies of my book? Would you have spotted it had you encountered it prior to reading this book? You're never going to be able to sell something if you don't convey confidence in producing whatever it is you're going to sell. Perhaps an emblem provides that confidence.

For centuries people have said it's not about where you start, but how you finish.

If you are dead set on pursuing business, then let the show begin!

Entrepreneurs often decide to start a business when they feel frustrated with the way life is working out for them. Do you often feel out of control? Do you feel as if you are suspended by strings and controlled by your corporate enterprise or by the expectations set forth by your peers? Or, are you the one holding the strings and manipulating your audience to do what you want them to do? Perhaps in parts of your life, you feel like the puppet, and in other areas you feel like the puppeteer. When you are holding something shiny in your left hand, are you distracting people from your right hand intentionally? Could it all be that simple? I will tell you that in business it is that simple, and anything you buy is a result of someone tricking you. Whether it's fancy packaging, mental manipulation with a perceived image you possess by making the purchase, or an irrational decision, somehow your subconscious led you to make a purchase. Have no doubt you did not make that purchase without influence!

The puppet show is something we are all a part of whether we want to be or not. What role were you born into? My metaphor in the introduction of the book was about life being one big rat race, but I also believe it is a perfectly calculated show. If it is, then this is how it works. There are those born as supporting cast members (like puppets suspended by strings). These people are content to work in a job for 60 years of their life and retire knowing they did a job well. The world needs people like this or we would have no one to implement our leadership plans of action. These people knew they did not have the "IT" factor long ago, and they settled with that reality. These people will not challenge the status quo, and they can easily end up behind the curve from where their ancestors left them. Those people will never come across this book as it is not in the section of bookstore they visit.

Yes, it's sad, but there are those that are just a prop inside the illusion. Like a red ball being shuffled around under a cup, never reaching their full potential, and never being more than what they were born to be. This is not okay!

Your one responsibility is to make sure you leave this world at least one notch higher than your ancestors provided you.

Faking it is a short-term solution.

Others will try to follow someone else's movements, but as the puppeteer, you know it's only you who can truly create change. Sure, you can hug the coattails of a colleague or a friend, thus not reaching for your own potential, and late in life end up having regrets.

Now that you see the world for what it is, don't you feel manipulated by what society presents as the norm or the expectations the outside world puts on you?

"Stay in your lane," they say.

I say, "Screw that!"

I got in the lane I wanted to be in, and I went as fast as I wanted to go. If you get in a lane you are not supposed to be in, then pretend you belong! I ignored the people who were sending me the message, *Do not resist the master when he or she is controlling your destiny.* Sometimes you've got to blaze your own trail and ignore the haters. Let the haters fuel you. This is the underlying message to the entire book and the underlying backbone of my story. Who is it who is telling you that you cannot achieve something? Or could it be that there are people intentionally trying to put obstacles in the way of your happiness? How does that make you feel? Does it further suppress your greatness or confirm your weakness, or does it drive you! All those people are controlling their portion of the show. How much longer will you let these strings get tangled before you cut them down with a machete?

Is today the day to recalibrate? Is it time to take control? Are you capable of handling that type of control? Do you feel like others were born into a better starting block than you? Were they born with the strings in their hands, or did they cut the strings and create their own destiny? I respect those who cut strings. I respect those who take control. Your peers are content with being suspended from strings and confined to what is socially acceptable. What destiny are they fulfilling? Aren't they simply running the race their ancestors started and holding that ground? They are surely not blazing new trails and new opportunities for generations to come.

Is that who you want to be? Is that how you want to be remembered? Know what your skills are, and work hard to recalibrate, fine-tune them, get out of whatever situation you're in, and knock down the fences. Set your goal, and your vision, and let's focus on how you'll achieve your dream. If you want to be an entrepreneur and aren't sure how, start by developing your sales and marketing skills. Prepare yourself to do the hard work it'll take to build the dream into reality. Prepare yourself for long, sleepless nights and extreme competition.

Great sales and marketing people are often great entrepreneurs. Bad sales and marketing people often fail at entrepreneurship. You must be willing to do the dirty work, and that means performing for an audience day in and day out, selling your work ethic and your goods or service. You can hire smart people, or technical people, but those who represent the show (the entrepreneurs, the CEOs, the leaders, the magicians) must be able to sell and market themselves.

If you aren't taking advantage of the loopholes on the path to becoming who you want to be, you're only hurting yourself. Wake up, and take advantage of the life hacks available to you through hard work and perseverance. Will you just follow the naysayers until the day you die—or are you reading this book because you want a way out?

Chances are you're tired of being a follower and you want to do a gut check on yourself and your ability to be a leader. Leaders cannot show they are scared or uncertain. **Leaders are fully committed to the path they have chosen and give comfort to those who choose to follow such a person.** Like a captain of the ship, you are the last one to panic in times of crisis and you are the only one with the plan. Think about being the leader! And if you don't think you need to hone in on your magic skills, think again. First ignite people to move in the direction you want them to move in order to build businesses.

How do you pull the strings and control those around you? How do you avoid being pulled into temptation or shortchanging your potential destiny? These are all important questions that we will touch on in the following pages, but know if you choose business, you're in it to win it. If you choose business, you have to be aware of your surroundings and learn to see the Sleight of Hand tricks that surround you every day.

3

Selling Magic?

In 2012 I had the privilege of meeting Zig Ziglar about six months before he passed away. For those younger generations, google Zig. Zig was possibly the best salesman to ever live on this planet. Or at least that is what his reputation would have you think. He was a terrific natural-born leader and in my opinion a damn good magician. I was blessed to have a one-on-one conversation with him that only lasted a couple minutes, but those minutes were invaluable.

Zig Ziglar once said, "No matter who you are or what you do, you are always selling."

So think about it! As a CEO, COO, salesman, or entrepreneur, all you really are is a performer. Hell, any job you do for monetary gain is most likely you putting on an act. How many people bet Peggy in HR is always Peggy in HR. When she goes home, do you think she lets her hair down, breaks a few social rules, and is turned off from being the HR performer she must be daily for monetary gain? Do you think Peggy wears a bathing suit at the beach or tank tops in 100-degree weather? These things are not acceptable in a place of work for an HR manager, but when she is not putting on the act, she can be herself. Every waking day, you are putting on an act; you are selling yourself to your co-workers, friends, family, and community.

Zig understood the illusion. Zig broke it down for what it really was: manipulating your audience. This sales process begins when you're a toddler. It starts when you want something to eat, and you have to convince Mom or Dad to get it for you. It continues when you're a teen, negotiating with your parents and teachers, and it never stops. When you go to your first job interview, you're selling yourself against other applicants whether you know it or not. Make no mistake; selling skills are vital to survive in this world. It's a survival tactic, and those that master it not only survive but thrive!

As an entrepreneur, every investor pitched or potential vision you are selling to your team is an act. Perhaps this is where I began to see myself as something more than a businessman. Only when you perform the act flawlessly does your audience believe what you are selling. To manipulate your audience is the characteristic of any good magician. Call it authentic influence, or call it great sales skills if you want, but I call it magic.

A salesman convinces a buyer they need their goods or services. Could they survive without it? Of course, but they need it because you convince them so. Is that not manipulating your audience? Is it really ethical? People sell by need, fear, and emotional reasoning, and by doing so are pulling the strings or delivering the subtle triggers that make someone say YES.

Through experience, I've learned it is all about "framing" and how you present something to your audience. For example, two competitive companies may use the same statistic or fact but in a different manner in regards to how they frame it to their audience. Imagine a diet product that claims, "Eighty percent of people taking the product have lost over forty pounds in less than a week." Then, imagine a competitor using that stat by saying, "The competitor's product does not work 20 percent of the time and with ours we guarantee results." Get it? The word choice pushes consumers' confidence in the direction you want it to go all by framing it differently. Neither of the companies is lying, but rather framing the words with the intent to deceive the consumer.

Are you relatable? Likable? Genuine? Believable? If not, you'd better figure out how to frame quickly. Does the product or service fulfill a need, solve a problem, or create hope? Desperation is not a good trait of successful salespeople or entrepreneurs. Yet a lot of times, especially early on in a startup, you'll be desperate even when no one knows it. There may be days where there's no money in the bank and your success is simply all up to you. **"Do not let them see you sweat!"** Frame the situation you're in to come off as positive even though you know it isn't.

If cash flow is tight, it's not due to the negative reasons that may be truth. Instead, tell the vendor a 50 percent influx in sales out of nowhere has unexpectedly tapped out your resources. See what I did there? If your vendors are calling and asking where payment is on raw materials, this is how you spin a time with low cash. You do not say, "Sorry we are out of cash right now and we will pay you when and if we get some again." You don't lie; rather, you reframe the situation to buy you time and give no reason for your vendor to question your ability to pull off the trick.

Remember the Golden Rule in sales: "People buy from people they like." People also extend terms to people they like! PERIOD. EXCLAMATION POINT! This book is proof you can convince or trick others to follow you and buy into your vision.

Does it really matter? It's all a play on words.

Think about it—even the most ethical businesses have their trade secrets, and their proprietary information. Everyone is putting on a show and trying to convince you to buy their product. The surgeon who buys the billboard that says he's the surgeon for "world-famous athletes on a sports team" is convincing you that you can be part of that exclusive club too if you choose his practice for your operation. His marketing is a form of sales manipulation, in order to make you feel better about yourself and your decision. The doctor did not think this advertisement up, but rather some marketing firm. Some business graduate was challenged to design a campaign that would deceive customers to pick a doctor they would not have otherwise picked without influence.

How much more credibility does one give that doctor than a doctor who has never worked on a celebrity? Should you give them more credibility? Probably not. What if that doctor was 99th in his class and his first surgery out of school was removing the tonsils of a nine-year-old kid who later becomes a mega superstar? What if that kid was LeBron James or Tom Brady? That doctor could say, "The doctor that operated on Tom Brady" on all his marketing materials, couldn't he? That is a SLEIGHT OF HAND in business, and they happen every day! It's about the tone, the delivery, the gray areas of the truth! Again, some business graduate took that fine detail and turned it into a Sleight of Hand; he or she framed it perfectly! It's not a lie, but was Tom Brady at seventeen the Tom Brady he became? As consumers, we don't know any better and we only see the smoke without realizing the mirrors are there. Look for the gray truth! This is how almost all business is done. It's deceptive and corrupt, but that's business. Learn to ask more questions. Try to seek out the Sleight of Hand in every situation and you may become a more rounded consumer.

No business flat out tells their customer how much profit they make off of a transaction, but believe me, they make a profit. For example, Southwest Airlines has a low fare guarantee. If your same flight is sold at a lower cost, you can contact Southwest Airlines and get the difference back prior to your departure. Southwest says they are a "transparent" company, their tagline being "Transfarency" in regards to their fair prices. However, in the fine print of their website, there are a ton of restrictions.

In 2018 a startup company got wise to code an algorithm tied to Southwest's website. The startup company had a subscription model of three dollars per month, and for that you would get an email notification when your same flight booked on Southwest.com sold for less, thus prompting you to get the money back they rightfully owed you based on their advertisement. Southwest did not like this and sued the startup company, which ended up closing its doors as a result.

Why did they sue? Was that too "transparent" for their liking? "Transfarency" is a manipulating play on the word *transparent* that a highly paid marketing team developed as the campaign and backbone tagline for Southwest, but they didn't truly mean they wanted to let the consumer know everything. This is where the fine print comes in. Apparently, the lawyers for this major corporation had already planned on someone doing this at some point as it was in the "terms and conditions" small font of Southwest.com that no external website could be linked to theirs for this exact reason.

How does that make you feel? Why do airline prices jump all over the place? Why if they could sell it for $200 a month ago, is it $1,000 the day before the flight? They will say it's a supply and demand thing, but seriously? Yes, I know the supply and demand game, but for Southwest, which lives off this "Transfarency" campaign, an honest world would leave the pricing at one set rate no matter what it is, with no jumping around. Do you fly Southwest because you have confidence in what they say is what they do? Does this change your mind about them? It shouldn't, but it should make you more alert to what every company does, in their own way, to get your transaction.

As you understand these basic rules of business, you will understand how I transformed myself from a blue-collar factory worker to market disrupter, from CEO to business master magician! You should be asking yourself if you are an entrepreneur? Are you capable of being a magician?

4

The Performer

By now you may be saying, *This guy's thoughts are crazy.* Or perhaps you're intrigued with how closely related my analogies seem to your life. By now you might start to think it's a sexier way to look at life and that being a magician sounds a lot cooler than being a businessman. By now you may think, *These are cute ideas, but what credentials does this guy have to prove his theories? Who is Dru Riess?*

In short, I'm basically a nobody but a humble nobody with an extensive resume. I'm cut from a different cloth than most of you (or at least society would want you to think that) and yet I see no hard evidence that would support why I would become more successful than you unless you simply don't try as hard. By now you should know that the will to try as hard and the ability to try as hard is where we are different. Talk is cheap, and no entrepreneur or upper-level executive lasts in a company if they are "just" a talker. Work hard, and don't just try. Try harder, do more, and work more than your competitors do.

In 11 short years, I built the best printing company the food packaging industry had ever seen. I had no formal training in the printing market, no packaging experience, no operating cash, and no business acumen. I was twenty-four when I started my company, and I was determined to become more than what I had been born into. Here are just a few local and national acknowledgments I racked up in those 11 short years:

- Featured on CNBC's *Blue Collar Millionaires,* season 2

- 2016 & 2017 *Inc.* magazine "5000 Fastest-Growing Companies in America"

- Featured in *Dallas Business Journal, Dallas Morning News, McKinney Magazine, D Magazine, UC Magazine, Voyage Magazine, Underdog NYC Magazine, Entrepreneur* magazine, and more

- 2016 & 2017 SMU Cox Dallas 100 list

- 2x cover story in *Flexible Packaging Magazine* as "2014 Top Printer of the Year" and "The Google of Manufacturing in America" in 2016

- 2016 Gold American Business Award

- 2017 Silver American Business Award

- 2017 Finalist EY Entrepreneur of the Year

- Quoted in several entrepreneurship books

- Featured on multiple podcasts, Facebook LIVE shows, and other media outlets across America

- 2017 *Entrepreneur* magazine 360 list "The Best Entrepreneurial Companies in America" #152 out the top 360 in the USA

- 2019 Tedx Speaker

By the age of twenty-nine, I became a millionaire, and by thirty I was a multimillionaire. I personally sold over $128,000,000 in packaging as the only sales rep for my company in 12 years. In other words, I know a little bit about selling, and about how to put on a show. I know about building a business and about being a market disrupter. I know how to be a leader, and I know how to develop an exit strategy. I know a lot about hard work, and I know how to manage and motivate people. The biggest and most important thing that I know is what it takes to break away from the preconceived notions the world had for my destiny. I don't know everything, but what I do know is exactly how to fulfill a vision and how to get people to see only what I want them to see.

Although I reference illusions and puppets a lot in this book, there is no magical formula for success. However, there is a formula. I am sharing my bag of tricks with you, my wins and losses, and I want to try to discourage you from thinking anyone can do what I did. Everyone can't. Motivational gurus will make money off of you or your friends by telling you that anything is possible, but it just isn't true. Can anyone be a supermodel? Not really, because you have to be born with certain physical attributes, like height and abs!

Can anyone be an incredible entrepreneur? Not really, for the exact same reason. There are specific traits you must have.

Let's find out what your traits are.

5

Trait 1: Vision

Everyone should have a vision.

Without vision, a magician would have no ending for a trick or there would be no originality to their act. What kind of show would that be if a magician tied himself up, dropped himself in a tank of water, and died? If you wander along carelessly without a vision, you run the risk of losing everything.

Vision is what pulls us in the direction of our dreams. Some of the greatest innovators in the world had only one thing driving them—vision. Vision is the big picture, the flame at the end of the tunnel, the hope that makes it all worthwhile and causes you to push forward on those nights when you're up working late and have more questions than answers. Vision is what Steve Jobs had before the iPhone and what he had when he introduced the tablet. Everyone expected the iPad to fail miserably as they saw no need for it. What's *your* vision? What is it that's pulling you in the direction of your dreams? Can you see yourself submerged in water, locked up with chains, and can you see yourself escaping for a round of applause? That's vision!

On day one of building my company, I saw a world-class production facility *in my mind* and a brand that would become nationally recognized. In the first couple of days in a steel barn in the middle of the country, I envisioned the day I would buy my competitors and merge them under my brand or perhaps going public with my company. Nobody sketched out a plan or gave me a Bible for food packaging to reference along my journey. It was instinctual. It felt natural, and it will feel natural for you too, if you're truly meant to be an entrepreneur or a leader. Steve Jobs was the entrepreneur; Steve Wozniak was not. Woz was an innovator at times, but today's "Apple" came from Steve Job's vision. Woz rode the coattails of Jobs and prospered for being in the right place at the right time. Without Jobs, Woz would be an average person working a 9 to 5 on the Geek Squad at Best Buy.

I remember speaking about my company out on sales calls in the beginning years, and what I described was a figment of my imagination. The facility and the way I described it was what I saw the company becoming, and not at all what it resembled out on that gravel road.

TRICK #1: Always lead people with a description of where you are going, not where you are or where you have been.
People want to know you're not done yet and that they should stay engaged for the big finale! I remember bragging about our company culture and what I viewed it as when only two or three people worked there. I was visualizing everything it would become, and it was natural. I was not selling packaging, but rather a vision. Not only did customers buy packaging because they bought my vision, but my employees bought into the passion I had when illustrating where we were going.

What's your vision?

At a time when I was only eating ramen noodle soup and Taco Bell bean burritos, I was envisioning a steak from Del Frisco's. When I started chasing my vision, I didn't drink alcohol, simply because I could not afford it in my weekly budget. However, a part of my vision was drinking the finest wines someday. No joke. Kanye West once said, **"Before I had it, I closed my eyes and imagined."** For a natural leader or entrepreneur, this is not a dream. This is VISION.

> *A vision for an entrepreneur or a leader is reality*
> *that simply has not happened yet. A vision to 99*
> *percent of the population is merely a dream.*
> —DRU RIESS 2016

Obviously, I do not respect Kanye for everything he has become as he is a prime example of someone who could not handle success, but as far as climbing his way out of his predetermined destiny, I respect him. Sure, I had doubts along my own journey, but I had a clear picture worth chasing and I believed in myself. You may wonder what synergies there are between Kanye and me, or even you and I. What is the common thread in us that makes us who we are? I can guarantee our values are different, and I can guarantee we come from different backgrounds, but both Kanye and I were fed up with seeing others control the show, so we made a dash for the main stage of our respected industries. How vivid is your imagination?

In short, I guess my vision was materialistic on the surface, but I assure you, all I wanted was people to notice me for me and love me for me. I wanted a wife to look at me like I was something special. I wanted kids to admire me and call me their hero. In my vision it was one day resurfacing on the radar to all those who ever doubted me, but with a grand entrance, perhaps a helicopter entrance to a high school reunion or something as simple as sending a signed copy of my book to a coach who overlooked me. I suppose in many respects I wanted to show people I could do it. For all the times someone told me I was worthless, stupid, too slow, too short, etc., I wanted to prove it to them—and prove it to myself too.

I often ask high school or college kids what their definition of "living the dream" is and they answer with a job. I mean I ask them; "what's your dream?" and they say being a lawyer at a mega firm downtown, getting a job in the Big Apple, being the Senator of Texas, rising up to be an executive of a company, or becoming an RN.

Wait, stop. Maybe I did not ask the question properly.

If the answers I am getting are work related, it may mean you're not aware of what the dream really is. I want to know what your vision is for your life. Who is there at your utopic ending? Are you married? Do you have kids? Where do you live? What will your legacy be? When you die what kind of impact will your life leave? Who will be at your funeral or will there be anyone there at all?

When you die does your story die? Who carries on the torch? Do they know your plan for the future so they can properly carry on your legacy? When I ask you what your vision is, answer me with a place that sounds like heaven on earth. Know your ending.

TRICK #2: Always know the ending to the trick before starting it.

It would look pretty dumb for a magician to grab a deck of cards with no plan.

Your job isn't going to be who you are. I'm not Dru the

printer, and you're not Andy the accountant or whatever your job is. Your vision is something bigger. It's the **end game**—the thing you want to earn money for and live for. Once you take the top hat off and hang up the magic act, where will the true you be? Once you know what your dream is, you can decide if you have the fuel to achieve it.

Know YOUR ending and then work backward from there to ensure that you fulfill your life. You have to know what your life looks like in the perfect light so you can recognize when you have achieved it. Your vision is not your work. It is not what you want to do for work. We are not put on this earth to work. Have you ever heard work to live or live to work? No one lives to work, so your vision should not be what you want your career to be. Your vision should be the LIVE part of the "work to live" saying. What are you LIVING toward?

I know people who are going through life right now who have no idea where they are headed. I work with people like that, I go to church with people like that, and I work out at the gym with people like that! I know people who are just living each day with no destination in mind. These people are followers, and followers typically let others pull strings and guide them because they have no vision.

Followers are those searching through a John Maxwell book for guidance on how to do something that is not natural to them. Get your head out of the book and go live life! You might want to wait until you've finished this one, but go live. Be the very best version of you and know why you were put on this earth. Find a purpose.

The best part about being an entrepreneur is the natural ability you should have to visualize your success. If you are unable to visualize yourself successful, I am confident you will never take the leap to be an entrepreneur.

Ask yourself now, Do I have a vision worth chasing? Am I

worth the gamble? If so, you should have a vision so clear that it is in 3D. If you have a vision, you should be able to talk about it and make others feel your vision is real. Like an illusionist pulling a rabbit from a hat or levitating right before your very eyes, you must be able to convince others your vision is worth having. The path or course you take to get to your vision may be fuzzy, but the end vision should be perfectly clear. You do not need to know how to fit the rabbit in your hat or up your sleeve. Just start with knowing you have a rabbit in your hand at the end of the trick.

Listen to me: **You are who you believe you will become.** Reread that slowly and let it soak in. **The better you are at performing and believing the statement, "You are who you believe you will become" the more success will come your way.**

6

♠

Trait 2: Motivation

What motivates you to do what you do, even when the going gets tough?

A vision is great, but it is only a picture of what you want to achieve. The motor to get you to your vision is the motivation inside you, but not the positive fluffy motivation that Tony Robbins or Darren Hardy sell you; nor is it the kind that John Maxwell pats your back with. I'm going to repeat this and I need you to read it slowly: THE MOTOR TO GET YOU TO YOUR VISION IS THE MOTIVATION INSIDE YOU! NO ONE ELSE POSSESSES A KEY TO YOUR MOTOR! It's not inside a self-help book, not inside a stadium listening to posers tell you about other people's trials and tribulations. "The only thing you will get from listening to people tell you that you can do something is a temporary moment of inspiration, not lasting motivation." There is a HUGE difference between being inspired and being motivated.

In fact, there is a better tool to use if you need instant inspiration; it's called music. Music will play a huge part in your success. Have those few songs you turn to in order to fill you up if you need a bit of inspiration, but understand a dose of inspiration and motivation as a whole are two different things. My songs—no joke—were "Hold On" by Wilson Phillips, "The Climb" by Miley Cyrus, and "Hate It or Love It" by 50 Cent. As cliché as these may be to you, Wilson Philips sang a song from my childhood that brings me back to a time I never want to relive, 50 Cent's song came out in college when I had nothing and wanted the world, and Miley's song came out the year I started my entrepreneurial "climb" in 2007. Remember, I started my journey on August 1, 2007, so these lyrics and the message of this song had relevant meaning to me more so than anyone else.

No one needs to be told how awesome they are! No one needs to be told they can do it! No one needs to be told how perfect they are! No one needs to be told they are special no matter the outcome!

It does matter if you win or lose!

When you lose, does it leave a feeling of emptiness in your heart that makes you want to fight harder the next time? In life, and especially in business, not everyone gets a trophy. Some get bankruptcy, some get a loss, some get robbed, some get corrupted. Millennials are in for a rude awakening due to how soft they are being parented and how this "equality for everything" plague has taken over our society. This is not a 10k run, and your friends aren't meeting you on mile 4 to scream from the side of the street, "You can do it!" My five-year-old could finish a 10k if she wanted to; it's the expectation. Sure, some may finish slower than others, but those positive words are not helping anyone achieve beyond normal expectations. This positive screaming from the curb is not the kind of motivation that is needed to create world changers, leaders, entrepreneurs, or trailblazers.

Yes, it feels nice when good things are said about you;

and it sure does sound good when it's coming from someone you admire, but if you want to change the world, this type of motivation will not get you further than your expected to get. Supportive motivation has no substance and only gets one mile per gallon. Think about it this way. You don't hold on to positive moments or nice things people say about you. You don't store away those moments and reflect on them when your back is against the wall, do you?

Dmotivation, on the other hand, gets 100 miles to the gallon! Who has ever done something worth remembering if it was the expectation? Name one! They call us 1 percenters for a reason—not because it was expected for us to achieve success. There was a 99 percent chance we would not make it, but we did. In fact, a study done in 2018 found that 53 percent of millennials expect to be millionaires at some point in their life. The catch was that none of them had an answer to how they would accomplish success. Rather, it was their expectation, and greatness doesn't come from holding your hand out, waiting for an opportunity to fall into it.

Imagine a basketball team up by 30 at halftime and yet they still lose the game. How does that happen? The other team does not miraculously become better, but rather the team with the big lead has an expectation now to win. The team that is down by 30 has internal motivation to show some pride, to prove their fans wrong who left the game at halftime, to validate themselves. And all of this is a form of Dmotivation. The drive, will, determination, and enthusiasm that the leading team started the game with has wavered, and they become content with playing the first half of the game to their full potential. They are content with the "glass half full" perspective! The team being doubted comes out and fights harder when it matters most and channels motivation from a place that few know how to on a consistent basis. The game is not over until the last second falls off the scoreboard, and no one remembers the halftime scores of any event. It's about wins and losses in the history books and not about the size of the lead or the odds stacked against you. There are no moral victories in business or in becoming more than the expectation for your life.

Was it Abraham Lincoln's support group that drove him to continue toward his vision? Was it Martin Luther King Jr's followers that kept him going? Was it Napoleon's friends telling him size doesn't matter that drove him toward success? Not one of these individuals did what they did because of their support group. Napoleon had something to prove since he was doubted due to physical restrictions like height. Martin Luther King Jr. did what he did because there were walls up in society where they should have never been and he wanted to be that guy to break them down. Millions told him he could not do it, but he pressed forward, relentless in his effort. The drive inside him was not fueled by the growing population that came in support, but rather the ideology that until every mind in America was changed he would continue on his mission. Thus, those who doubted him or disagreed with him were his fuel!

Shaquem Griffin is an NFL football player who was drafted by the Seattle Seahawks in 2018, but unlike anyone that came before him, he is the first player without a left hand. Do you know how many other fantastic athletes there are in college football who from first glance should be better than Shaquem due to not having that limitation? Did you know Shaquem's brother plays for the Seattle Seahawks as well? What are the odds both would make the NFL or that they would be on the same team! Growing up, do you think people told him he would never make the NFL? Do you think people were in his ear telling him his brother was a better candidate to make the NFL? Limitations and all when channeled the right way and used with the right perspective can fuel an individual to greatness.

Brian Dawkins was an NFL Football player inducted into the Hall of Fame in 2018. In Brian's speech he thanked all his haters for fueling him his whole life!

When motivational goons sell you a glass half full, they are telling you to look at the positives in life. The entire motivation market has been oversaturated for decades with corrupt, selfish, and clueless individuals selling nothing of substance and selling the wrong perspective. Most motivational speakers do not speak from personal experiences and they sell what the crowd wants to hear—a feel-good story! I'm not here to make you feel good. Looking at the glass half full has and always will be the wrong way to look at how to motivate anyone past expectation. If your glass is half full and you did nothing to get the first half of water, what would drive you to do something for the other half? The result is millennials with their hands out waiting for Mom, Dad or someone to come by and fill up the other half.

When someone with drive and determination looks at a glass half full, they feel ripped off. My question is, "Where is the rest of my water?" Shaquem's question, Brian's question, Steve Jobs, Abraham Lincoln, and so many people who achieved greatness did not see the glass half full. We wanted our glass completely full, and that means living your life looking at the glass as half empty. Looking at life in this perspective allows you to create change and drives you to fulfill your full potential. If you want to channel your motivation that will fuel you to greatness, look at the glass half empty and figure out what the hell happened. What is required of you to get the cup full!

I see people spending time and money on resources for

inspiration, motivation, guidance, but they are all being sold false hope. The motivational goons we have in the market today sell you fluff and words jam-packed with preservatives and artificial ingredients. Words are all they are selling with no meat on the bones.

Once again, if you're having marital issues, depression issues, etc., use all the resources you can to get your mind right again. This book is about figuring out whether you're meant to be a world changer, trailblazer, rainmaker, entrepreneur, or divergent. This is a business book, and like all things there are exceptions to the rule.

My Thread Theory: Motivation, Part II

My **THREAD** theory is that Motivation begins as a piece of thread. If you think about a piece of thread and compare it to a thick braided rope you should notice the tensile strength between the two. While the piece of thread would snap with little force, the thick braided rope could hold hundreds of pounds of force. The average person needs to be motivated or inspired to accomplish even the smallest task. An entrepreneur does not. An entrepreneur, world changer, divergent individual is self-governing by nature and possesses self-autonomy to stay accountable. Even the smallest task being completed means something to a person who is self-governing, and that means no loose ends. That means no one has to be watching for an entrepreneur to do what needs to get done. If this is not you, then I think you answered your own question of whether or not you have what it takes, and we are only getting started.

The thicker a rope is braided, the more it can withstand. To prove this theory, I took a piece of dental floss and tied it to a 10 lb. weight. I lifted the weight by pulling on the piece of dental floss, and the floss snapped instantly. I then took five pieces of that dental floss and braided them together. I tied the floss around the 10 lb. weight and lifted the weight five feet off the ground effortlessly. What if I suspended the weight of my body onstage with a thick braided rope? What if I did it with a piece of floss? Don't go into business without a strong enough backbone or a strong enough rope. It only takes a handful of Dmotivational threads to fuel you to success. You can have more or less, but processing threads in the correct manner could be the difference between a life of mediocracy or a life of greatness.

Ask yourself if you have insecurities. Ask yourself how you got those insecurities. We are not born into the world with any insecurities; rather, we are given each one by outside influencers. In today's world outside influence is impossible to ignore as social media can reach you anywhere and at any time. Social media is setting the expectation for what is right and wrong, but is your goal to live up to their expectations? Did someone make a comment about the way you look when you were younger that has stuck with you to this day? Did an outside influencer have anything to do with what type of swimsuit you wear or if you look good in hats or not? Did someone make you feel less for not wearing name brand clothing as a teenager and you still yearn for their approval in your thirties? Ask yourself how many threads you may have encountered in life that you possibly did not process or use them in the correct manner? Did something tragic happen to you and you lean on that memory as an excuse rather than a crutch to move you forward? Did they hurt you or motivate you? Can you feel these threads when you reflect on them? If so gather them together, tie them together, and give it a pull. How supportive do those moments feel when collectively put together and channeled in the correct manner?

When someone Dmotivates you or puts you down, what

filing cabinet do you put that in? Consider the top drawer the drawer of Dmotivation. This drawer is where you take hurtful or Dmotivational moments and process them for fuel. This drawer is where you hold on to those moments and use them to get you where you want to be in your vision. The bottom drawer is where you file things for revenge and resentment that will rot you from the inside out. Let's keep the bottom drawer as empty as possible! Use everything to gain momentum in your journey, and the less baggage you are pulling around in the lower drawer, the better.

In your darkest moment as an entrepreneur or as a leader, I promise you that you will not reflect on Tony Robbins, John Maxwell, Dru Riess, your mom's kind words, your favorite coach who was supportive of you, or some nut job as your fuel.

Sure, other people's stories may help you realize that if they can do it, you can too. But when I hit my darkest hour and my success was on the line, what I reached for was the most hurtful insult I may have ever gotten from a peer. I reached for my rope! Maybe it was someone telling me to have a backup plan. Maybe it was someone telling me I was wasting my time. Or maybe I reflected on a past time when I failed and had that sick feeling in my stomach: *If only I would have tried a little harder.* Look, failure is fuel. Missed opportunity is fuel. Tragic moments of loss in our lives—fuel! The pain from the loss of a loved one—fuel! What would that loved one want to see you become? Is it worth shattering expectations in remembrance of them?

What about moments when you didn't know if you could do it and you doubted yourself so much that you got stuck? Fuel. Look back at yesterday briefly, but then use it as the fuel to compete today. Let failure make you stronger. Perhaps you recall a time a loved one broke your heart or someone you looked up to let you down. In your darkest hour, that is where you find your motivation! All of those moments woven together make your Dmotivational rope. All those tiny threads woven together create your backbone for success.

Some people don't go through a lot in life, and yet they want to be something amazing when they grow up. The silver spoon kids often fall flat or fall short of what their successful parents were capable of doing in life. The reason for this is because they have no backbone; they have no rope. Those that can harness that anger, that resentment, that disappointment, and store it away as fuel for when the time comes are ones that will rise up and get through their darkest times. Each thread is a moment in your life that built you into the motivated individual you are.

When I was in first grade, I was put into a Catholic elementary school. The annual Food for Fish drive was done in the fall, and me, being a selfless and loving kid, wanted to contribute. (For those that don't know, the Food for Fish drive is a food drive to collect nonperishable goods for the homeless.) I had recently had a goldfish as a pet at home that passed away in a relatively short amount of time. Don't they all! At any rate I had a ¾ full can of fish food on my shelf in my room that I had no plans of using anytime soon. Being a giver, I put the can of fish food in my backpack and brought it to school the next day. I handed the can to my teacher and told her I wanted to help the homeless, so I wanted to donate "Food for Fish." As a child, I had no idea how that was going to help the needy, but I did what I could to support the cause. The reaction I received from that teacher and the kids in my class is something that hurts me to this day. The children laughed for what seemed hours, years, decades, and the teacher told me I was not very bright; and I stood there in disbelief.

Moments like this are demoralizing and Dmotivating!

These moments prove we are human as we feel pain and embarrassment. Where does that pain go? Mine went into a reflection bank of memories that I pull from until this very day.

I once had the privilege of hanging out with Ron Hall (*New York Times* Best Selling Author and professional philanthropist) and I was explaining to him my theory about Dmotivation threads. He lit up as I explained my theory and smiled. I asked, "What is it?" He replied, "I, too, have several of those moments I reflect on still to this day."

Ron was in his sixties when I sat down with him, but one of his most visible Dmotivational threads came from his second-grade class. It was common in those days to have a cup sent home with you after school by the school nurse. The next day you were to return with a urine sample for disease testing. Ron returned the next day and placed his cup of pee on the teacher's desk. His teacher walked into her classroom and saw a cup of urine on her desk. She asked, "Who's is this?" Ron answered, "Mine!" Ron was proud he remembered to do what was asked of him and returned it just like he was asked to. Or did he?

The teacher then said, "Well, it seems Ron is stupid and can't follow instructions." She continued by saying, "Ron, all the other kids listened and dropped off their urine cup at the nurse's offices on their way into school today, but you are apparently stupid and can't follow instructions." This hurt as you can imagine it would. It was embarrassing, demoralizing, Dmotivating, and enough to scar him forever. The teacher made him miss recess, and in front of all the other kids, she insisted he stand outside on his tippy toes with his nose against the wall of the school building. While he was elevated on his toes, she drew a circle where his nose touched the wall and told him if she saw his nose come off that wall, he would miss recess the rest of the week.

This was his punishment, but what the teacher did not notice was the impact she would have on the rest of his life.

Year after year we collect these moments of hurt, disappointment, pain, Dmotivation, and it's how we reflect on them that make or break our chances for success.

As I said before, I am not on this journey with you, and though some of my philosophies or ideas may seem relevant, you do not need me in your darkest hour. You do not need anyone else to pick you up. You need you! You need you using those put-downs to lift you up! You need to know your "WHY." Why are you doing what you are doing? THE MOTOR TO GET YOU TO YOUR VISION IS THE MOTIVATION INSIDE YOU! You need to know your motivation, and you need to push toward that vision harder and harder.

Once again, motivational speakers are selfish. They care about only themselves, and they think you need them to get you through your darkest hour, but that is so far from the truth. Remember, the glass is half empty, not half full. You only need you when you're an entrepreneur as you're already a 1 percenter for trying to become one. Entrepreneurs have the backbone and the resources to channel their internal drive. I'm not special; just a regular guy who pushed through all the criticism, haters, doubt, and did it.

You need to be there with you along your journey in good times and bad, so use the tools you have. Realize this is all just a show. You have all your props and tools, all your ammunition within your heart and mind. Tap into yourself and pull yourself toward your vision, and when pulling isn't enough, then push. Do whatever it takes! Don't read this book to be motivated; read this book to find parallels in your journey and possibly learn how to handle a situation I have encountered that you are bound to encounter. If you think, *I may not have what it takes*, then you're probably right. If you find you have the threads it takes, then you owe a lot of people these two words: *thank you.* "Thank you for being tough on me, thank you for doubting me, thank you for settling as a prop in the show, and thank you for the fuel!" Take the time to thank those who hated on you, doubted you, fueled your insecurities, caused you pain, and more. Look at the glass from this perspective! Without these moments and without these experiences, you would not have what it takes to potentially reach success. Does this Dmotivational thing make sense?

Random thought

In 2000 there was a fantastic movie with Eugene Levy called *Best in Show*. It was a comedy based on stupid humor about dogs in a dog show, but there were two lines in that movie that made my college buddies and I crack up for years. Whenever we would leave a party or event and say goodbye, we would recite these lines: "If you get tired, pull over" or "If you get hungry, eat something." How stupid! Seriously, is this not common sense to anyone else? If you find that remotely stupid, then why do millions follow people like Tony Robbins?

Here are some real quotes from Tony Robbins:

Identify your problems, but give your power and energy to solutions.

Your past does not equal your future.

Things do not have meaning. We assign meaning to everything.

What the f---? This guy is absolutely the dumbest individual ever! Did he have a concussion when people asked him for these quotes? I nearly choked in laughter when my wife read me these few quotes while doing some research for my book. I immediately had a flashback to college with my buddies mocking the movie *Best in Show*. My wife and I both can't understand how in the world people follow a guy who says common sense stuff like this. Really! To be fair it's not just him, it's all motivational speakers that speak without speaking from experience. He has no originality to him, yet finds an audience to prey on. Is this the kind of guy you are seeking motivation from? Do you see you're probably looking at motivation in the wrong perspective and probably following the wrong kind of person? It's not about fluff motivation; it's about Dmotivation.

Thread #1

So, what created the monster inside me?

Why was the fire in my belly so huge?

I started at the bottom.

I felt like the ball under the cup—and I was determined not to stay there. I came from middle class parents who were too young to be married or have kids. I was an accident, and they made it very vocal that I was an accident my whole life. (Thread #1.)

Thread #2

There was no money for my parents to pursue a higher education, so my dad joined the air force to pay for college. My mom wasn't left with any other option other than to stay home. Imagine an eighteen-year-old girl, with a new baby and a shotgun wedding, living on a military base with no chance to further her education. My mom spent her life working odd end jobs, from being an administrative assistant, jewelry associate, interior design assistant, or anything that she could find to do for work that didn't require her to have any type of education. I know that seeing that early on was the stirrings of the fire that drove me. I didn't want to feel limited. Inside I was limitless. This was thread #2.

When my sister was born five years later, my life changed. My first life memory is the day my sister, Karen, was born, and it's forever etched into my mind. I remember holding her in the hospital when I was five and running down the halls screaming, "I have a sister! I have a sister!" I didn't realize then that we would be linked forever. I would become her guardian and protector for life.

Thread #3

Looking back at my parents' relationship now, I can see that they should have never been together. How many people do you know like that today? People meet for a variety of reasons, whether it's need, fear, lust, or money and decide unintentionally to build a life together.

My parents were young, and they no doubt felt stuck raising two kids who they never planned on having. They fought every day, screaming and yelling at each other over money and life. This taught me a lot. Remember when I talked about fuel? Nothing like your parents arguing about money to make you certain that you'll never lack money or argue in front of your kids. There were no happy memories of my childhood with family other than spending time with my grandparents. I have great memories one-on-one with each parent, but for me to recall a family memory where we were all together is not feasible.

When I think about my memories, I am reminded of days and nights hiding in my sister's closet with her Care Bear sleeping bag wrapped around our ears so we could muffle the sounds of the fighting and screaming.

Our whole childhood was "forced family fun." During the holidays we would take pictures, and I can look at those images now and remember the fight that happened before the image was taken. "Shut up and smile," my mom would say.

Because of that, I have the fuel to create a much different life for my kids. Nothing about their childhood will be fake. Never will they look back and remember the days when they had to shut up and smile because they'll be smiling for real. It's funny because people ask my sister about memories of her childhood, and she can't really recall those bad moments. In essence I did what I was trying to do, which was to protect her from it. My role was her protector, her guardian, her big brother, and I knew I couldn't change the way my family was, but that I could protect my sister as much as a little boy could. I watched over her the way I always wished our parents would have watched over us both.

Thread #4

I can't blame my parents today, as they are good people who did the best they could do, but they both made decisions that made their life harder than it needed to be. They were two parents trying to figure it all out on the fly. My parents could not afford daycare, so my sister and I were forced to go to work with my mom during a period of our childhood. At the time, she was the secretary at the local YMCA. Her responsibilities began by opening the gym at 5:00 a.m. During those summers we woke up at 4 a.m. and my mom put us in the back of our Jeep Cherokee equipped with our Ninja Turtle and Care Bear sleeping bags. We either slept in the back of that Jeep or on the hard lobby floor until 6:00 a.m. That is when people started to arrive at the YMCA for the day and we could not let it be known that we were unsupervised with our mom at her job, so we had to be invisible. My mom's boss could not know we were there. This may be the first moment that I learned how to be a magician. I learned how to hide and how to operate the system.

My sister and I played together almost every day, shooting hoops, playing on the gymnastics equipment on the third floor, or walking around the small town of Piqua, Ohio, by ourselves. We felt bad asking my mom for money, as we understood the value of a dollar. I remember it being a treat when I was allowed to order three things off the Taco Bell menu. At this time bean burritos and soft tacos were 50 or 69 cents each, but we were always on a budget. I was a kid, and I did things I'm not proud of during those days to get by. Because my arms were skinny, I would steal from vending machines so my sister and I could have a snack. I probably stole over 100 honey buns from the bottom row.

We used to go around the city of Piqua, Ohio, and scrape for change under any and all vending machines. We had a route we would do and could typically score a couple of bucks. It still baffles me to this day how much money we would find on a regular basis under Coke machines. It also embarrasses me to think about what others must have thought when I was laying on my belly on the side of the gas station where the Coke machines were scraping for change. What were the passersby thinking? How embarrassing that was! It's experiences like this that I truly believe contributed to my desire for success and gave me that "IT" factor that so many pretend to have. The "IT" factor is not something you can buy. It comes from an inner drive to succeed or die. If you don't succeed, maybe you won't eat. If you don't succeed, maybe you'll end up like your parents. None of those things were ever an option for me.

Like many people, my childhood shaped my mind and the vision that I had for a family someday. Even before I ever had a wife and kids I knew one thing: it would not look like my childhood. It was something that became so tangible in my mind. Even in these unhappy moments, I could see what life would look like someday. My vision of what I knew I wouldn't do was growing. I've since learned that it's not uncommon for kids who have less to want more for their families.

Thread #5

I tried hard to be friends with guys in that city, but they clearly saw me as competition. Competition for starting line-ups in athletics and competition with girls as my personality was off the charts compared to theirs. Yes, I was a dreamer and actually had a vision for my life compared to their lack of, but they cut me down and made shrewd comments about me while in a crowd of people to make sure I was beneath them. Some of the harshest criticisms about my physical features and my manhood were said in the most inappropriate times by guys I thought were my friends, but that's life. I didn't go shoot up the school, but rather stowed that pain away for fuel later in life.

Thread #6

Like many, I have faced rejection several times in my life by the opposite sex. I can't count the number of times a girl I thought was pretty gave me a cold shoulder. I'm talking fifth and sixth grade, I'm talking seventh and eighth grade. These are influential years in your life when you form your personality and your self-identity. My self-esteem was very low for a long time, and that definitely fueled a fire from within to compensate for my natural shortcomings with success.

Thread #7

Despite the way my parents started out, my dad climbed the corporate ladder and has been an engineer at an aerospace company for over 25 years. My dad was a good dad despite hating his marriage. He spent time with both my sister and me and coached our sports teams when he could, and he wanted badly to see us become famous in that small town, in athletics, and in life.

I was an athlete since the day I was born and played everything from T-ball to soccer to football. My dad was there pushing us all the way. I was good too! I was better on the field than most, yet I was overlooked in my small town. This town was divided into different family cliques. It was a bunch of people who grew up together, still smoked pot with each other in their forties, raised their kids together, divided sports leagues into SELECT teams, and chose whose children could play together. It was never based on talent. New families coming into town had to play in the rec league or at the YMCA, and from that experience, I learned early on that in order to get somewhere, I was going to need to play in their puppet show. This is typical small-town America!

Have you ever had to be fake to fit in? Never being chosen despite my skill level meant I had to think differently. It took years before I formed some fake relationships with those kids and earned my way onto the SELECT teams. The forming of those hollow relationships in middle and high school was the beginning of the show for me. It was how I started cutting the strings that were controlling my future in sports and in my life and started being the puppet master instead of the puppet. As soon as I moved on from that small town, I never looked back, and I have zero contact with anyone from high school, as I knew those relationships were fake. In fact, I changed my name from Drew to Dru after I left high school and have never had a Facebook account or any social media in my life. I never wanted anyone from that city to have contact with me again and so far so good!

Despite making the varsity team, when it came down to the bright lights and being able to show my talent, I learned that being on the varsity team didn't always mean you played. I resented being overlooked and was often bitter knowing that I was a better athlete than the third-generation kid who weighed 140 lbs. and was scared to catch a ball across the middle. I was five feet ten and 170 lbs. I never dropped a ball in practice, but I never got an opportunity in the game. I played several meaningful minutes, but only when my team was desperate. It was because of these experiences that I swore to myself I would be heard. I gained more clarity for the vision that I wanted my life to have by being looked over. I knew that when I surpassed this little town, I would make sure I was never someone who ignored someone smarter or more talented than me just to get further in a game, in life, or in business.

Thread #8

When you begin to think of the fuel, negative or positive, that are the defining moments in the way you think about life, you can start to see the threads that drive you. As I grew into a young man, I watched my parents worry over money and struggle with conceptually achieving their goals or getting to the end picture they had for their life. I was reaching for more, and at one point I found guidance in a girlfriend's dad. At fifteen, I entered my first relationship and stayed in that relationship throughout college. That was a good solid foundation for me to study, grow, and learn from.

I've often learned the hard way how there's learning in every situation and every relationship along the way. The relationship itself was not the value for me long term, but the parents of that girl were the *game changers* for me. I have found that often relationships don't show their true value until they are over and reflected on. In this high school relationship, I saw how her parents were in love and how they showed love to their children.

This pure love taught me a new model for what a relationship and family could be. Her dad was smart, and he would coach me without me even knowing I was being coached. I guess as I have a daughter now, I can see why he was willing to coach a young man who was close to his daughter. I don't know if he knows it to this day, but his message got through to me. He was a finance guy and taught me about financial responsibility, and he taught me how to treat a woman and how to love a daughter. After three years in that relationship, I had grown equally close to her parents and felt like between my dad's side of the family and these two individuals, I had a great support system going away to college. Their guidance was why I made my vision come true.

Look for the angels in your life. Family isn't the only place that you can gain perspective and knowledge for making your vision a reality. You can look for other role models in your life to show you how to get up and make things happen. Don't miss those moments to sit by a fire and chat with them.

Thread #9

Two weeks into my freshman year of college, I got a phone call from my mom. My mother (never innocent in her own right) was hysterically crying, and then the crying led to screaming and the screaming turned to violence. My dad had cheated on my mom with a woman at his workplace. Eighteen years of marriage done! It didn't surprise me that it was over, but the way it ended is something that I would have never imagined and I will never forget. I never thought of my dad as a guy like that, but he made a huge mistake. This one event started a chain reaction in my sister's and my life that would change the way that I looked at family forever.

I rushed out of my dorm, grabbed a friend's car keys, and blazed the 80-mile difference between my hometown and the University of Cincinnati. Not to rescue my mom or dad, but to check on my sister. My sister was turning thirteen at the time and being a teenager is already hard. This was serious, and she confirmed what I heard on the phone when I talked to my mom. I approached the house to find my father begging for my forgiveness, pleading with my mother that he would do anything to make it right again, crying with eyes full of regret. Those looks and those moments are burnt into my soul.

My first thoughts were to drop out of college to raise and protect my sister. Do I move with my mom to get away from this cliquey hometown where the "other woman" was well-known and liked? Surely my mom's time in that small town was over. There was no way my sister could enter high school with the "other woman's" son being her same age and not get teased. My mom would get glares and people would judge her or talk about her. These moments are the ones that can change the path of your life.

Thread #10

I knew more than ever then, that it was my sister and I against the world. Do I drop out of school and raise my sister alongside my mom? I reached out to my girlfriend's parents at the time for guidance. They had been a stable rock in my life, and I had been dating their daughter since I was fifteen.

Her dad was always a hero in my eyes and his advice was invaluable.

"Dru, you have to stay in school," he said. "Just finish out your freshman year, and then figure out what you want to do."

I had always listened to him, because I could see how he took care of his life and how he raised his daughter. He had written the letter of recommendation that helped get me into college when all the universities I applied to denied me for academic reasons. I took his advice, and I made the choice to finish. I know that I am the man I am today because of the time that he invested in my life.

My mom packed and left quickly for Orlando to at least get close to her broken family and as far away from that small town in Ohio as possible. My sister moving across the country from me was the hardest part of my entire life to this day. The person I felt responsible for like a father since the age of five was now 1,000 miles away and it hurt. The guidance I got from my girlfriend's parents was to stay in college, keep doing me, everything will be fine. As hard as it was to hear it, I trusted them and their counsel so much that I listened. That choice to finish propelled me forward in college. I worked even harder to be more than where I came from.

Thread #11

My parents' endless fighting and their eventual divorce taught me an important lesson about how important vision is. My parents never had a vision for what they wanted their lives to be. They also didn't have a plan once they became parents. They spent every day just fumbling through their lives unintentionally and made important life decisions on the fly. Never planning, just moving through life with the only purpose of paying the bills and surviving. I knew that my vision for my family would be planned. As an entrepreneur, you must have a plan and the ability to execute the plan.

I told my mom and sister that I would make everything right. I was going to get rich and they wouldn't have to worry anymore. I said this every single time I saw them for the four years I was in college. I always left them by repeating, "I'm going to get rich and everything is going to be all right!" I had never in my life made a 3.0 GPA, and my first quarter at UC I did. I was a 1.9 to 2.0 student in high school, and books were not my strong suit. Did I mention that every college I applied to denied me, but through some begging and letters of recommendation from certain individuals the University of Cincinnati took a chance on me?

I believe the world is made up of book-smart and street-smart people. I was street smart! I would take street smarts over book smarts any day. I had my mind made up that I would do this by myself. I would grind, bleed, sweat, and do whatever it takes to become something. I wrote music and performed all over Ohio, Kentucky, and Indiana. The music was my quick shot to get rich, and like many artists, I knew it was a long shot. I dealt with people constantly telling me they didn't like my music, I dealt with people telling me I would never make it, and so on and so on and so on! There were more people who gave me positive feedback than those negative naysayers, but the positivity doesn't stick with you! The people who liked me and wanted my autograph were not people I can put a face with a name 15 years later. However, those that went out of their way to tell me I would never make it have a lasting image in my mind. The positivity doesn't stay with you!

The music was also an outlet for my anger, because it was a place to express myself, and I recorded an album called *Whatever It Takes* by the time I was twenty.

What I did not notice was that playing music onstage in front of hundreds or thousands of people, night in and night out, was also breaking down walls in my social ability. I honed in on a skill set and polished my comfort level in front of people. Every great salesperson and every great leader shows no sign of nerves, and I wonder to this day if the music was God's plan for me to perfect his greatest hidden treasure within my DNA.

TRICK #3: Learn to mask fear and only show the audience what they want to see and hear.

Was music a hidden way to fine-tune my motor skills as a master magician? I have ice in my blood like the greatest magician, and my desire to perform only intensifies when an audience is watching.

I could cold-call Warren Buffett with no remorse. I do not get nervous; I get anxious to see the result of every sale I go on. Until this day, I have never heard NO. That does not mean people have not told me NO; rather I have elected to not hear it. A NO to me just means "not right now," but I eventually always get them. Entrepreneurship takes persistence and the ability to shake off rejection. Some people just need a little more convincing than others, but stay persistent at your craft and you will convert every indecision into a YES.

I continued school, performing music, and working at several restaurants and factories during the summer. I worked for Coca-Cola's shipping docks for three summers, Children's Hospital in Cincinnati for two years, PF Chang's, T.G.I. Friday's, and an assembly line in a steel factory all while holding down a full-time school schedule. Things with my band didn't pan out. We got close to a record deal but it fell through. In other words, one path to my ultimate vision closed and I was left to blaze a new path.

In 2003 I was flipping through a course book at the University of Cincinnati, debating what to minor in. I was twenty and getting my four-year bachelor's degree in Business Administration, but had to choose something to minor/major in. All my prerequisite classes were done, and it was time to pick the nuts and bolts that I would offer the world when I left this institution.

A friend of mine said he was going to minor in a new entrepreneurial program that had recently been added, and for whatever reason, I decided to join him. Up to this point in life, I had always been what my family considered a dreamer. I was an aspiring musician convinced that fame and fortune were around the corner for me. In the back of my mind, this college stuff was a waste of time, but I went with the flow and did what my peers were doing. I was always scheming and looking for the easy way out.

As I started the two-year minor program, I found myself interested in the classes because they pulled my creative side into play. No, it was not music, but there was something about executing a business idea, writing a business plan, developing a product, and marketing it just right that was very similar to the stimulation I got when composing music. Being an entrepreneur is being able to think in a way that not all people think. It is a mind-set that allows you to see weaknesses and exploit those weaknesses in a current market; or it gives you the ability to conceptualize a brand-new product/market need. I was arguing endlessly with my professors as I pitched off the wall ideas that they were too dense to understand. My senior projects ranged from an indoor snowboarding park to a ski resort business completely indoors in even the hottest climates to a breathalyzer app that allowed your cell phone to tell you if you were too drunk to drive.

KEEP IN MIND, THIS WAS IN 2003 and 2004—apps had not been invented back then! Keep in mind, in today's world there are now indoor snowboarding parks, as well as ski villages, and the #1 shark tank idea is a breathalyzer app! Impressed? You should be. I was that forward thinking that I thought of how to utilize a device that everyone in the world possessed or soon would possess and how to use it for more than just communication. Apps as we know them today were invented when the smartphone was evolved in the iPhone in 2007. IBM claims they invented the smartphone in the 1980s, but they just want the exposure. Had they invented it, they would have made it available to the masses. In short, the entrepreneur thing and the visionary thing was so natural to me. Finally, I predicted or pitched to some investors in 2006 that cupcakes were going to be a new fad and that we should open a store that only sold cupcakes. In 2005 there was a company in Beverly Hills known now as Sprinkles that has now become a massive success nationally. I had never heard of Sprinkles, but clearly I was onto something. Today I can go to every shopping center in Texas and there is a cupcake store of some sort.

In short, the entrepreneur thing and the visionary thing were so natural to me. Being an entrepreneur is so much about feeling the market and anticipating the consumer's future needs. For most entrepreneurs the first idea will not be the one they are successful in, but how many times is a songwriter's first song the hit song that makes them famous?

The things we were learning about in school were relative to any business, but getting an A in all of the entrepreneurial classes available will never qualify you to be an entrepreneur.

To recap: Can a non-entrepreneurial person still pass an entrepreneuial class with an A? Absolutely. Does it mean they can be an entrepreneur? No! Why? Because it is about what fuels and drives you, and it's about having that "IT" factor. Being an entrepreneur is most often a matter of the heart. It's an inner drive and creative vision that often ignites and defines the journey. The type of entrepreneur I best relate to is the "street smart" entrepreneur.

The "book smart" guys are often good inventors, creators, tinkerers, but not entrepreneurs. There is an element of street smarts needed in any entrepreneur as there is no manual that comes with building a company. Do you have street smarts? Do you have common sense? Are you self-governing? Street smarts is a matter of having common sense and fixing weaknesses where they need improved upon with simplistic solutions and not overthought and overanalyzed reasoning.

In 2005 I graduated and moved to Chicago to try to weasel my way into an advertising firm. I went straight to Leo Burnett, one of the most renowned advertising agencies in the world, and I was going to get myself a job. I saw the movie *What Women Want* growing up as a kid and I wanted that job. I wanted to build brands, I wanted to create slogans for Nike, write jingles, or help build reputations. However, I was never even given a conversation. My name was nothing; my resume was a bunch of hourly jobs I had grinded at to provide for myself since I was fifteen. Other kids I went to college with got better grades but had never earned a dollar in their life. Oddly enough those kids landed good jobs right out of college. But how? Their parents' connections! Of course, maybe it was unrealistic to think that I could waltz into the largest advertising firm and among millions of recent graduates get a job. However, I did know a silver spoon kid with no work experience whose grandfather knew Leo Burnett, and getting a job at the firm came really easy to her. It was clear that nothing was ever going to come easy to me. It was clear the kids in lane 1 were still running the show. It was obvious that Mel

Gibson was sixty years old in that job for a reason. Those jobs are not available until someone dies or retires and you have wasted your best years on the sidelines.

Positions like the one Mel held in the movie *What Women Want* was one that takes decades to climb into, and I was not going to wait around for decades to get where I wanted to be. Rejection often ignites entrepreneurs even more. I simply pocketed the anger and said to myself, *Okay, I'll be back.*

Thread 12

The reality is that after graduating from college you have very few options. Enterprise Rental Car seems to be the most popular company for hiring entry-level graduates, but that's a joke. They tell you it's a stepping-stone to getting experience on your resume, but in actuality it's a waste of time working at an undervalued job that ultimately dead-ends. Impatience is a great gift for any entrepreneur. Again, push for results and when they are not coming fast enough, push even harder! I wait for nothing, and if people can't keep up, I wait for no one as well.

To add to the defeat of not immediately landing my dream job at Leo Burnett, my seven-year relationship with my girlfriend ended. My immaturity and inability to trust others pushed her far away. I know this was rooted in my parents' split because I was always looking, reaching, and wanting approval from others. I take full responsibility, but I was yearning to feel like I belonged somewhere. In that moment, I lost a great friend, and in that same instant I lost my role models in her parents. It was a hard season of life.

One of the things I learned from it, however, is that it's really true that whatever doesn't kill you makes you stronger.

Thread 13

It's cliché, I know, and it's probably advice I would hesitate to give my own children. I know from experience that during hardships you really just want someone to listen, because during hardships you are not looking for advice. These clichés only make sense weeks, months, or years later. I would also learn years later that everything really does happen for a reason. And, if you're an entrepreneur and need to make things happen, it's going to take work, ideas, mentors, support, and confidence. In life there's always going to be personal obstacles such as a breakup, but you've got to pick yourself up, dust yourself off, and keep on living. When you lose one mentor, move on and find another! Don't forget the wisdom that has been poured into you, but build upon it. What would I be if I had stayed in Chicago? I would be a puppet!

Fate led me to Colorado and then on to Texas; and this path led me to make millions, then settle down. You have to be open to change, you have to put your ear to the ground and listen for your calling.

When Chicago continued to have nothing for me, I decided it was time to move. I was looking for a job and I found one in Colorado, which was a district manager for a payroll company. It was lower on the totem pole than I ever anticipated for myself, but it was better than Enterprise Rental Car. So I packed it up and moved to Colorado Springs. I needed to refocus on my vision and reroute myself. I just didn't know how I was going to do it.

I moved to Colorado with optimism that everything was going to be okay. Despite having put myself through college, the breakup, combined with a mediocre job, had me sitting at rock bottom mentally. I had no guidance and no support system other than a homeless dog I found on the streets and took in on my travels out to Colorado. I had walked into Leo

Burnett and they laughed at me. I had called and emailed my resume to at least a hundred other positions.

A voice inside myself told me, *What are you even doing this for anymore? You aren't going to become anything, Dru!* I started to believe it. I became a nomad. I considered moving back to that small town in Ohio and being another number. I was that guy who I despised with a lack of vision. I would go snowboarding three or four days a week, and I wasn't applying myself at the job I had. I was basically just coasting by and collecting a paycheck. Underperforming at my job led to tension between my boss and me, which ultimately led to me being unemployed.

With a college degree and the understanding that life isn't free, I sucked up my pride and went to the Colorado Springs PF Chang's to get a job. Yes, it was again embarrassing to have a college degree and stoop back down to something I was doing when I was in college, but bills still had to be paid.

I was waiting for some kind of miracle to happen. I was alone and I had a choice. Curl up and die or dig deep. I wish I could say I immediately chose to dig deep, but instead, I went into a deep depression. I wouldn't eat at times, I would overeat at times, and I would sleep for days in a row for months.

I finally had a life-altering moment at the end of 2006. It was snowing, my dog had died, my grandfather had passed away, and I was spending Christmas by myself in a small apartment in Colorado. I was broke, my two credit cards with 27 percent interest were maxed out, and I couldn't afford to fly to see my sister in Florida. I walked outside on Christmas morning, I was in a pair of basketball shorts and a short-sleeved shirt, and I stood outside behind a white wooden fence in the freezing cold. I looked out over the Garden of the Gods in Colorado Springs. (For those who don't know what it is, google Garden of the Gods). I was cold, yet couldn't feel the cold, and I sat down in the snow crying. I probably cried for 30 minutes. I could not feel the wet snow as I sat there. I told myself in that moment, *Go inside and end your life. What do you really have to live for?*

When I had asked myself this question in high school or college, I always had an answer. *My mom, my sister, my girl-friend, my friends, they need me.* This time the only person who I could come up with was my sister. I had realized that any relationship or bridge I built in college had been burnt from my immaturity and lack of respect. My mom had fallen out of my life, as she made choices I did not agree with, and the girlfriend's family was long gone. My sister was it, but was it enough?

My dad's family chose to distance themselves from me at this particular time and chose to welcome my dad's mistress in as family instead. This made it awkward for me to attend any family function, holiday get-together, and more when they would gather in Cleveland. The fact that I had a sister was really the only thing that totally stopped me from doing it. If I had no sister, I guarantee you I would not be here today. I can guarantee it! I sat there and had a conversation with myself. I can vividly remember these words:

You do realize that this is the worst it can ever get?

Sitting there in the snow, on Christmas, I had to laugh about it. My tears turned to hysterical laughter and then back to tears. Was I losing my mind, or was I gaining a grip on my life? Did I just process this situation all on my own? I felt like the Joker from Batman. No counselor? No peer? No support? Was I becoming Neo from the matrix? Was I seeing life in an alternate perspective that few have the ability to see life as?

You do realize that this is the worst it can ever get? I repeated.

Every step from this moment forward will be improvement, I thought. I went inside and, like most people do at one point or another, looked at myself in the mirror while I was crying. Zig Ziglar says, "The eyes are the mirror to the soul." I starred at that mirror and soaked in the look on my face, and I stored away the image of what that kind of pain looks like and feels like. I stored away the emptiness and the feeling of being all alone. I vividly can recollect on this moment for a defining thread in my life, and it's all I need as motivation.

Note: Today it is harder than ever to motivate myself as I have accomplished more than most would in two or three lifetimes, but when I reflect on this moment, it's all I need. Motivation to me comes natural as I know how to use my threads without any effort. Experiencing this low is the reason I am still reaching for more and have the fire of a LION inside me to not just win, but win big. It's easy to be complacent and to get stagnant. Keep competing for as long as God gives you the ability.

Then I repeated: *This is the worst it could ever get. So why not see what tomorrow brings. It literally cannot get worse.* I was talking to myself in the mirror!

The following weeks I started binge-watching reality TV. I would watch a lot of MTV reality shows like *The Hills, Eighth and Ocean,* and I started to make up an alter ego in my mind, a confident persona that was capable of blocking out how bad it was at the bottom. I was poor, had no car, and no opportunities, but I had this newfound confidence. Maybe it was here in this moment that I tried on the top hat for the first time and became somewhat of a showman. I started to walk, talk, dress, and style my behaviors after these rich kids in California/Miami that I had never met, but that I saw on TV. I was becoming a performer. By spring I had met another young guy at my apartment complex with bigger dreams. He was new to Colorado and fresh out of college as well. However, he was book smart. He was an engineer and made six figures a year, but he talked about wanting to be rich someday. He read a lot of books and would meet up with me on the weekends to talk about these Rich Dad Poor Dad books he was reading during his travels for work.

I told him I was going to start a business, and I pitched him an idea and he bit on it. He was making more than enough money, so I suggested he be my financial backing. He suggested we become business partners in my idea. I was the idea guy, I was the engine, I was the vision, I was the motor, and he just wanted to be a part of it. To this day he tells me he knew there was something about me, something he believes people call THE "IT" FACTOR. Oddly enough I had a close friend in college look at me one night and say the same thing. At the time I did not pay it much attention, but as it came off his lips it came out in slow motion. I thought, *"Do I? Do I have an "IT" factor?* I thought so, but was there truth to it? What was it that these outsiders were seeing from me that had them vocalize it?

If there's one thing you can learn from my story no matter how old you are, it's that when you run out of options, you've got to reach out and find another option; find another thread to hold onto. Don't show all of your cards and allow people to think the trick is over. A great magician reads his audience's level of engagement, and if they are not impressed or perhaps no one is watching anymore, recreate yourself! Reach for inspiration! Don't just sit around all day playing video games or wandering aimlessly. This is critical when the chips are down and you feel like life isn't ever going to go your way. Keep on pushing. Never give up. Like a magician, find the trap door! There is always another way out.

In the end my threads were a strong enough backbone. No, these are not all my threads; some of them were too embarrassing and personal that I could not bring myself to put them in this book. But I'm sure anyone reading this can understand. How many threads do you have? Do you want it bad enough? Are you motivated beyond the point of no return with the right type of fuel, with Dmotivation?

My Ricochet Theory of Life

Let's talk the Ricochet theory. This is my theory for how we end up who, where, and when we become who we are. From the ages eight to twelve, you form your personality. This is truth. This is not my personal opinion, but rather science. From eleven to fifteen you form your identity, your sense of self. Who you are born to be and what you are born into is pure and raw. As we discovered two chapters back, when you are born, you have no insecurities, you have no hate in your heart, you have experienced no ricochets, and you have no will to win. Sad, but true. The feeling of loss and the feeling of winning do not exist at birth. Through experiences, good and bad, we learn those pains and joys. We are all a reflection of our experiences in life. Unfortunately, outsiders influence us during the most critical years, and that sense of self is actually only 20 percent us and 80 percent what others have made us feel we are or have to be through ricochets. Every experience, good or bad, has an effect on an individual. What happens when you experience your first heartbreak? Have you ever heard of the rebound? Rebounds happen in more events than just a relationship. Every pinnacle pivot in our life leads us to ricochet or rebound to the next best thing at that current/particular time. Most of the time it's not even the next best thing, but rather the next thing. Maybe it's a substance, maybe it's an individual, maybe it's a task or circumstance you fall into without thinking.

The definition of a ricochet is to bounce or skip with or as if with a glancing rebound. When you are broken up with who do you turn to? Whose arms do you fall into? When someone cuts you down, but then the next person lifts you up, the next person puts you down, and the next person lifts you up with a compliment, how do you process the polar opposites? How does your mind transcribe these events and process them? How do you bounce from one emotion to the next? Is the positive enough to counterbalance the negative, or does the put-down trump the compliment? With all the outside influences, especially during critical years, you are constantly ricocheting off of things. Emotionally and mentally you are bouncing from one experience to the next, ultimately landing you at the age of eighteen and graduated from high school. Then what? Maybe you did not graduate high school due to a ricochet that was not recoverable and led you down a path of self-destruction. Did you get in trouble for underage drinking? Did that cause you to get kicked off the high school team and eliminate any chance of you going to college for athletics? Did you get in a car accident and accidently kill a friend and that detoured your life's output? Did you fall into drugs and waste away critical growing years? Did you get someone pregnant or get pregnant yourself, thus putting a speed bump in the way of your maturing process? Have life's ricochets led you to college? Have your experiences sharpened you and made you who you dreamed of being as a little kid or are you playing the ultimate game of "keeping up with the Joneses" (trying to be accepted by your peers)? Your identity is oftentimes not who you would have become on your own, but a fraction of that person. Knowing that you now compensate for areas you are weak with an act, what does that do to you?

Imagine if while building your business you avoided potential ricochets? I did. For my business, I did not need social media, as I will mention several times in the book. By doing this, didn't I cut off an outlet for any criticism or outside influence to reach me? In today's world, our kids are connected to technology at such a young age through social media, video games, and more. If someone wants to reach our kids, they can, and if they want to say something hurtful, they can. During those critical years of influence, their sense of self and their personality are not original due to this. They will second-guess themselves as people's opinions instill doubt in their minds about their abilities. While building a business I had no social media presence, which allowed me to avoid unneeded and unwanted ricochet moments. If you had something to say to me, you better have my email or cell phone number. This is called being laser focused and aware of what ricochets can do. While I believe in using Dmotivational moments for fuel, I did not need any more, and I wanted to put my efforts toward making progress toward my vision. Nothing was going to derail me on my mission!

Let's take two seconds and leave the book of business for a moment. Let's talk life. Since I have an audience, let's talk about processing the impact of ricochets. Like anything being beaten on, it eventually gives. The mind, the body, a cement block is not built for constant impact. Yet we ricochet all day, every day, year in and year out. Life is hard and it's hard enough without others, negativity or disbelief in your goals. If you, your kids, your loved ones could only process those ricochet blows the way you do Dmotivational thoughts, perhaps we would have fewer suicides and school shootings. If a kid trying to find their identity was put down by a peer or made fun of for a physical feature, that often ignites a "get even" thought process. Let's teach others how to bounce off even the worst moments in life and realize there should be no value given to others' opinions of who you are.

Ricochet off of and away from those who are not good for you and process the event in a way where it fuels you instead of anchoring you down. Sound familiar? This is how my Ricochet and Dmotivational theories meet in the middle. When you lose a loved one or a tragic event happens in our life, where do you bounce to next? When you experience a setback or have to choose from an undesirable choice, how do you pivot? What chapter comes next in your life? **No more getting even, no more guns brought to school, no more violence, but instead prove your better!** The common theme to my advice is to use things that others see as trash as your treasure. When a team loses a championship game, they come back the next season fighting to get back to that moment for a chance at redemption. I have never heard of a team of competitors losing a championship and then all committing suicide because of it. Yes, it hurts, but so does breaking your toenail! Everything hurts in the moment of hurt, but process it and know that life goes on. Know there is something else out there that you will bounce off of or onto. Perhaps it's a worse situation, but the hope that it might be the right situation for you must be there as well. As my current mentor says, "The sun will come up tomorrow." Control your ricochets when all seems lost. Get up and realize not all seasons are good in life, but we can rebuild and move on. Tomorrow always brings something more, and you deserve to see what it has in store for you.

As an entrepreneur, the hills, peaks, valleys, plateaus, and more will be enough to break you mentally. If you keep a foundation of knowing tomorrow is a chance to bounce back, you will lead people with a steady hand. As bad as today may be, your tomorrow in the life of an entrepreneur is a spring-board ready for impact. Ricochet off the bad days, events, experiences, and toward the direction of your vision. Pull and push toward your vision with the Dmotivation, inspirations, motivations, etc. You are the motor to get you to your vision; you and no one else.

Don't Feel Sorry for Yourself

This is a short chapter that basically reminds you that feeling sorry for yourself gets you nowhere. Believe this: In business no one feels sorry for you! No one. Would you perform for an empty room? No. Why feel sorry for yourself? No one will be there with you, so while you sulk, pout, or cry, no one else will be. You have two options at all times. Move on or quit! Either get over it and keep grinding toward destination SUCCESS or don't. Don't feel sorry for yourself when a customer stabs you in the back. When an employee stabs you in the back, don't feel sorry for yourself when you don't get what you want materialistically. If you want something, go take it, but you can't do two things at once. No one can. So either pout or get up and go make progress.

I know this is some common sense stuff that some motivational guru would tell you, but for crying out loud there is no other way to say this. Stop feeling sorry for yourself and your situation.

Core Values

Your culture and character are just as important as your product in the market. Your culture is your reputation inside your own walls. Make sure people know why they show up to work toward your vision every day. Every company should have a simplistic mission statement, brand promise, and set of core values that any-and everyone can remember. In the beginning, I made the mistake of having too many core values and thus no one could remember them; so no one lived or worked their day with them in mind. Yes, I admit I made mistakes along the way! I later revised them to define who I am and what I wanted our company to be remembered as long after I'm gone. I reflected on our youth, our tenacity, and our uniqueness as the new company in the industry. I realized we were Gen X's first representation in this industry, and I reflected on that pinnacle moment when I got a "GRIP" on my life staring into that mirror. We were a generation of fist-bumpers, crazy handshakes like LeBron James has with his teammates, and hang 10 sign language around the press room. From this reflection, I formed our Core Values around the fist-bump. When you close your fist to fist-bump someone, you are making a gesture of gripping something. Thus, our Core Values are rooted in the acronym GRIP: Grateful, Reliable, Innovative, and Passionate! These are the four things I was relentless at being and I have kept as my compass during my time as an entrepreneur, magician, husband, father, and friend. I'm forever **Grateful** for God's gifts and those who allow me to do what I do. I'm **Grateful** for those building this vision with me and I treat people that way. I am known and any company I am associated with must be known for being **Reliable**. I would die before intentionally letting someone down. Through the years I never stopped **Innovating** and improving upon processes, procedures and pricing, strategizing, and creating the work environment we all participated in. Lastly, as an entrepreneur, you have to keep your spark. Your **Passion** is what ultimately draws energy from others and attracts customers to do business with you. As an entrepreneur, you can never lose your passion. Once you lose the passion, you're dead in any business environment.

In 2015 I was so **Grateful** for the guy who gave me my first order back in 2007 that I shoved thousands of dollars' worth of cash into a FedEx box and sent it to him randomly. It was years after he gave me that order and he was no longer in our industry. I tracked this guy down to his current workplace, and on a random day he received a FedEx box at work. He opened the box and nearly fell out of his chair. With that cash and a personalized letter, he smiled and rushed home to show his wife. He has no idea what he did for me and my future family's legacy, but I hope he gets a sense of how appreciative I am. I later found out he bought a new motorcycle with the cash, and I'm proud to have made that happen for him. This was only one of a thousand things I have done for people since coming into success, and you have to stay grounded and continue doing things like this throughout your life. It's the reason we are put here! We are not put here to be actors, although that is what it takes to make it in this world. **"Acts of kindness are the only things that make us feel truly human."**

In addition to your customers, your people deserve to feel your appreciation. Keep it loose and give back. Give bonuses when you can and give them often. Be visible and do the small things like engaging in conversations with them on a personal level, and hand out full-size candy bars once a month to your entire company. I mean you personally hand them out one by one. See the difference it makes! Do raffles, play games, keep it fresh, and you will reap the rewards.

The reliability of your product or your commitment is what gives a buyer peace of mind. Remember these words: "YOU ARE ONLY AS GOOD AS YOUR VENDORS." This goes for you and it goes for your customers. If your vendors suck, you look like you suck, thus perception is reality. If your vendors are rock solid, they put you in a position to kick ass and take names. You have to be reliable, and there are no excuses for sucking. If your vendors suck, get rid of them, move on, find better vendors. Don't allow yourself to suck! Be reliable even if it pushes you near death. Even if that means missing nights or weeks at a time at home with your family. Even if that means all-nighters being pulled. Be **reliable**!

Along the way you have to look to continually improve yourself and your company. Without improving upon mistakes or weaknesses, you will be a temporary success. Without improving you will be limited and the ability to scale your business will be impossible. You have to be **innovative** and never take your foot off the pedal while building your business. Keep the show fresh, keep the audience anxious, continue introducing elements of surprise!

Finally, wear your **Passion** on your sleeve. Make it visible that you have a purpose and that you're willing to do anything to meet or exceed expectations. If you do this with finesse, you will come off as someone reliable come hell or high water and your passion will be taken as a positive trait. Harness the passion and disperse it as needed. Core Values are things that should be reciprocal. The most ideal and the rarest relationships are those that your customers value you as much as you value them. If you can get your customers to be these four things and you be these four things back to them, then you will be nearly impossible to stop.

Do you remember Willy Wonka? Do you remember how elaborate his tour of his factory was? Use his inspiration when building your brand and your culture. Channel his spirit. Be quirky, be different, be unique. Do you remember being excited about seeing what was coming next? Wonka was a natural showman. From candy-coated wallpaper to bubble-filled weightless rooms. How would the next child be knocked out of the competition? Does it correspond to how a business can get knocked out of the competition? Remember Verruca Salt being **ungrateful** and "wanting it now," but then being flushed down the golden egg tubes? Remember Mikey TV being shrunk to the size of an ant for not listening to simple instructions? Do you remember Augustus' lack of self-control, which led him to fall into the pool of chocolate and nearly die in the drain tubes? Each one of these scenarios can be related to business.

Don't be ungrateful! Have discipline and do not get tempted to sway from who you are. It will be tempting at times to make a quick score on customers in a pinch or customers less knowledgeable. The best way to build a business is to be disciplined and push greed out of your DNA. Be Charlie! Be the Charlie your business needs and have a "GRIP" on who you are and who you want the business to portray. Have humility! Listen to customers' needs and solve the problems that your customers are speaking of. So many business owners hear the customers, but they are not listening, which ultimately means they do what they think is best. A lot of the times your answers are right in front of you. But far too often pride, ego, bad habits, and loss of self interfere with making the right decisions.

In my twelfth year of building the business, I brought in a Senior Vice President (Jack) who had over 35 years of experience streamlining production plants. He was only with me for a year, but that year was a year of growth for me. As we began to know each other, we would share war stories from our life's experiences. I was thirty-five, and he was in his sixties, but many of our professional experiences were parallel. I learn a ton every time I sit down with this man, and one of my favorite stories is a story he tells about being grateful from the beginning of his work life and beyond.

The story goes that his boss at one of his first jobs sat some production guys down in a room and told them how much he appreciated their hard work and how he wanted to reward them. Jack had not been at the company for a long period of time and was shocked this man wanted to reward him. The man said he would be giving everyone in that room (about ten guys I believe) ten-cent raises. The room had a mixed response. The guys groaned and moaned, sighed and blew off the gesture. The man was taken back. However, Jack's response was to go shake the man's hand and tell him how pleased he was to be there. Jack thanked the man for his job and realized this man did not have to give him ten cents. In fact, the man does not have to give anyone anything, but he did. Jack's enthusiasm and counter-reaction to the rest of the guys had his boss retract his offer to the other men in that room. He said due to how ungrateful the others were that he had a change of heart. Rather than give everyone ten-cent raises, he took all the dimes and gave a dollar raise to Jack.

See the difference in how someone can react in a situation where being grateful should have been everyone's response? If this characteristic is one that is naturally in your DNA, you have better odds than others to be successful, you have better odds to sell customers and attract people to want to follow you. If you don't have this in your DNA, learn to be an actor, as you will have to present yourself as grateful in order to get anything positive in this world.

People who work hard and achieve higher than expectations are eligible for bonuses in life, but they are not guaranteed and you should not feel entitled to one. If you have a job, do the job to the best of your ability every day. Don't do your job expecting something more in return. You were hired to do a job. Be grateful you have one. These are core values within you, for your company, for your life to abide by, so get a GRIP!

7

If the Hat Fits, Wear It!

Most entrepreneurs have an idea or start a business from ground zero. Most get funded or fund the businesses themselves in steps and phases. Most people start businesses in fields they understand well and have an idea of what the market is lacking or needs improved upon and they take their knowledge and they grow it into their business.

My first business idea was one that I believe I was an expert in, my first idea was starting at ground zero, but that business never got a shot to take off. It wasn't 30 days into working with my new business partner that another opportunity came up. In this regard my story is a little different, but first things first. I had to accept the role as the master magician. Maybe the fact that I became an entrepreneur in something I had never heard of and made it a mega success is why my story is worth telling. Maybe the fact I took on a business not at ground zero, but far below the core of the earth drowning in debt is why my story is worth telling.

In 2007 my business partner was traveling to Dallas for work and met a Real Estate Developer who was ultra successful at developing master planned communities. Like most cocky entrepreneurs they assume they can be successful in any industry once they have been successful in one. You will come to find out the hard way this is not true. The odds of a startup business making it is slim to none. They say a business that is in business for two or more years is a huge success! If you are fortunate enough to be successful with one of your startup ideas, don't try to do it again! What I mean by that is "NOW stay in your lane." If you do get tempted to start another business at some point, stay within the scope of what you were successful with the first time. Keep the next ventures complimentary and close to the nucleus of what made you successful in the first place.

For example, I was successful in printing food grade packaging so for me to hypothetically go and start a design firm that specializes in producing brands artwork for food grade packaging, would be a great fit. For me to branch off and start a contract packaging company that fills, blends, and produces packaged food would be a great fit. But for me to go and start a tech gaming company is bound to be a failure. Don't get too cocky and think you're something special. Realize who you are and be grateful for your win.

You can keep winning by making smart decisions, but that starts with setting boundaries for yourself. Set boundaries for your investments and be disciplined with who you choose to let get close to you who may sway your decision-making.

In this case, the Developer reached too far outside his comfort zone and in 2006 had purchased a printing company in St. Louis. The Developer knew nothing about blue-collar grit (he went to Northwestern for crying out loud), he played basketball at Northwestern, he was the whitest guy in the world, and he knew nothing about manufacturing. He purchased the company and never traveled to visit or had any interest in the business. Eventually, over the course of 12 months, the company died for lack of leadership, poor management, culture, and business acumen. The Developer mindlessly shut the company down in St. Louis but had all the assets moved to a piece of land located 40 minutes north of Dallas, Texas. The land was farmland with a green steel shed and two classic red barns. The moment he shut down the food grade printing facility in St. Louis and moved the assets into a barn located off a dusty gravel road, he basically dug his own grave. He tried once or twice to revive the company by hiring people off recruiting websites, but nothing stuck. Thus, the opportunity to rebuild became available for me. In 2007 I signed a sweat equity deal on a napkin that promised me 49 percent ownership in the company if I could get the old owner (the Developer) out of a half million dollars of personal guaranteed debt.

The opportunity was to build a printing business in the food packaging industry. The problem was that we had no clients, no experience, no working capital, and no business plan. I was twenty-four years old, I was emotional, I was desperate, and I had nothing to lose.

The day I chose to take on this opportunity is the day I stepped into the role of entrepreneur and immediately felt the pressure.

The process of becoming an entrepreneur, and the everyday life of an entrepreneur, feels like you're the magician standing on the stage preparing for his grand finale. The day-to-day life feels like being handcuffed and lowered into a glass casket filled with water.

Every single day feels like this! The key is thrown to the bottom of the casket and the lid is sealed shut with padlocks and heavy chains, then covered with a large cloth as the audience waits. This feeling never goes away until the day

you retire, sell the business, step down, or die. This is the best analogy there is for someone who goes all in on being an entrepreneur. If you know someone who owns a business or is self-employed, ask them if this kind of pressure is the pressure they live with every day! Does this sound desirable to you? Even if your business is soaring, I promise this is the anxiety you will live with every day. Think about if that is the life you want.

Sure, the ideology of controlling your own schedule sounds nice, making more money than you can spend sounds cool, but are you that naïve to think that it doesn't come with a price? Think about any celebrity or rich person who has taken their own life. You look at the story and think, Why? Why would you do that when you had it all? Why would you get addicted to that substance if you had it all? But did they have it all, and how do you cope with that day-to-day life? Why weren't their weaknesses visible to those close to them? Why didn't someone help them? Why? Well, because they are magicians and they don't show the parts of the trick that are not desirable. Fact! For whatever reason, no one likes to show vulnerability or weakness, and part of that is because "no one feels sorry for you when you're on top." Thus, you are left on an island to process success and the baggage that comes with it on your own.

You don't know what you don't know. You don't know what external pressures come with success, but you'd better ask yourself if you're mentally strong enough to handle life-or-death stress day in and day out before becoming an entrepreneur. Entrepreneurship comes with baggage, but for whatever reason, we don't talk about the hard times or we skim past it quickly when telling people about how we achieved our success. The pain and suffering are the guts to how success was possible, but people want to hear the Hollywood story and not the reality. Will you struggle to unlock the handcuffs and get out of the casket without drowning? If you do struggle, how will you compose yourself during the struggle? Will you ever stand on the stage again or will you die? Will you enjoy the prestige of success? Or the doom of failure? Every day is unknown in the world of entrepreneurship and you're only worth your latest success.

As a magician, the next audience wants to see the trick and does not care what you did the day before or what you do for someone else. You have to bring it every day! You have to bring it for your peers, your employees, your family, your customers, etc. Each day is a new act and all eyes are on you. I had the vision to see this company built and to see it profitable, but I didn't know how I would do it. I had no education or experience in the printing or packaging industry. I had no allies or contacts in this century-old industry. How in the hell would I build a company based on something I was clueless about? There were many moments where my oxygen was low. I felt like I was in that glass casket struggling. On top of that, the fear would set in and I would wonder if I could really pull this trick off.

Only you can hear your thoughts when you're in that casket. You're the only one that can slow down your breathing. Only you can slow down your heart rate and gather your thoughts. You're the only one that can assess the situation and find your way out. There's nobody else in there with you, and no matter who you surround yourself with as you build your company, the pressure will remain the same. That's the life of an entrepreneur. Do not allow people to ever see you panic. Would a magician let you see him panic?

There were a lot of trials and tribulations along the way. I had just turned twenty-four years old, and it was a Hail Mary pass to think I could come in and pull off the impossible on my first attempt at being an entrepreneur. But I guess at twenty-four I was somewhat of a SHARK to take 49 percent equity in a guy's company without putting a dollar into it. That or this guy was desperate and he put his last dying wish in an unproven kid with tenacity and grit. There were nights I sat at my desk with my head in my arms and fell asleep. Those were the nights I truly felt like an entrepreneur.

I knew how to sell, and getting the orders seemed to be the easy part, but don't forget we had to learn how to run the machine and master the science of flexography. Several variables stood in our way, including what ink systems to use, and what manufacturers to partner with for press supplies, and how to use accounting software, as well as learning the difference between 100 structures that looked the same, but performed differently for certain applications. With all of this going on, a costing platform had to be figured out to make sure we were covering all our costs and capable of making payroll—to name a few major obstacles that played against us. Not to mention no working capital (meaning no money in the bank to begin with). If I wrote a book about the story and about the painful times, I would have to write a separate 70,000-word novel. For everything to click and for me to learn what I needed was a miracle.

If there was any chance for us to succeed, we had to be profitable from the first job on. The only way we made payroll is if we made enough profit to support it. (And I skipped several paychecks!) The only way we paid for raw materials was if we had profits to pay for it. The only way we made a capital investment in new equipment or improving the barn facility was if we made a profit. Talk about having your back against the wall! I guarantee there is maybe only .000001 percent of entrepreneurs that actually start this far in the hole. Someone starting a tech company is probably pretty versed around technology, probably pretty good on computers, and understands what they are trying to provide a user when launching their company! I have never heard a story of anyone pulling off what I pulled off, and I guarantee it does not exist. Over the years I have been told and I have come to the conclusion that I may be one of only two people if there is another person on this planet who could have pulled off what I pulled off. I say that from the humblest place, but it is fact. Think about it. Industry knowledge was at zero, debt was over negative $500,000, and we had no operating money, an inadequate facility, extreme competition with over 3,000 other companies doing what we do in the United States, and more. One slipup and it was over! This forced me to be far more strategic than a guy who raised some beginning capital on Kickstarter or went to a bank for a business loan. People that raise money like that are not in debt when they start, and they also know a little bit about what they are about to embark on.

Remember, respect is earned and not just given to someone for having a title! I worked hard and earned respect. I let my employees see me sweat right there beside them day and night. A piece of advice: *Don't hire people to hire people. Don't be lazy. Understand that long hours and multitasking different roles come with the job of being an entrepreneur.* I have never hired someone because I wanted to create a department or a position. I have never hired someone because I did not want to do a certain task. If we wanted to start a position, we would do the job ourselves until the job became a full 40 hours or more per week. We would multitask until it was beyond humanly possible to sustain that role. My advice is to be absolutely sure there is a full-time position there before hiring someone. For nine years I prided myself on not having to lay off anyone, as every position we hired for was a position that was needed and gave value to our P&L.

It was three months into the project and the Developer extended the rebuild project another 60 days. For the first three months, I was able to miraculously pay the rent on the building, pay the lease payment on the printing press, and pay my two employees' paychecks by the skin of my teeth. On the weekends I cut the grass around the 20-acre farm, as we could not afford for someone to do it and it had to be done. Cutting the grass was extra work that took up about seven hours of my Saturday, the Texas summer heat was unbearable, and I did this just to not add more fixed expenses to the business. *In addition, it's probably why at thirty-five years old I had the beginning of melanoma removed from my back, but sacrifice is everything when building a company.* By being frugal and pushing my body past its breaking point, I was able to keep the company afloat. Yes, I worked seven days a week and had no social life. Get used to it! This is what it takes.

The sales were achieved by using competitors' websites and piecing together a few lines of BS that made me sound like I knew what I was talking about. This is street smart! A book-smart person would not have thought to do this, as it was too obvious. I owe a lot to stupid competitors who put glossaries of industry terms on their websites and put pictures of their actual customers on their website. I mean, how stupid can you be?

I grabbed short terms and phrases that I saw on their web-sites when researching my industry and repeated them like a robot. I sounded the part because I used terms like "EAA tie layers" and "Light, Oxygen, and Moisture Barriers." I had no idea what I was referencing, but it made me sound credible. If you can talk above your audience's understanding of the industry, then you will become the smartest guy in the room, but at the same time know when to keep your mouth shut. Again, common sense but something someone street smart possesses. From my three largest competitors I would say they are 50 percent of the reason I am standing here today. I stole their customers by cold-calling them, and I used their own industry knowledge from their websites to combat their sales process. *Glenroy, Belmark, Labeltech, and others, I owe you a huge thank you!* Thank you for not educating your own sales team enough and for allowing me to educate myself by using your resources. I guess I was hungrier than your best salesperson, as no one could sell against me when it came to technical expertise for the product.

Your tongue is the one gift that can make you sound dumb or sound intelligent, but sometimes the ability to control the use of your tongue makes you appear as the smartest guy in the room.

In the first two months of building the company, I decided I needed to expedite the learning process, so I went on to Alibaba.com and networked via chatrooms and email with packaging printers in Taiwan, Singapore, and China. I took my personal credit cards and booked a trip to Asia by myself. I was scared. I won't lie, but being twenty-four years old and going to remote areas of Asia by myself scared the shit out of me. I remember landing in Singapore with no idea how to communicate and no idea how their currency worked. I navigated my way around the city and toured two print manufacturers while I was there. Each facility in Singapore had a translator, and I performed an act that would have won an Oscar. I told these manufacturers that I had about $30 million worth of business in the States that I was looking to move overseas to expand my profit margins. By dangling that carrot, I was treated like royalty as I was escorted to and from the airport.

From Singapore I traveled to Taiwan, as well as three remote areas of China. When I say remote, I mean *remote*. I saw rice fields and people harvesting the fields. I saw warehouses that literally said "Sweatshop" on the outside of it. I went so deep into the hills of China, roads ended and turned into dirt roads, where manufacturing facilities were more like prisons. I could have been killed, robbed, held captive, but I risked it all.

I performed the same act at each location, and in total I toured seven facilities that showed me how a print shop should look, act, flow, and operate in the food packaging market. During this trip, I saw things that 90 percent of my American competitors had never been exposed to. Think about this! Are you willing to take such a risk for your own business? I could have died. I could have been robbed and left stranded in a foreign land. I took that risk! I risked my personal well-being, but all for a greater vision!

When I returned from this trip, I could intelligently discuss how film was blown, the differences between rotogravure and flexography print science (the two print sciences that service my industry and the difference between domestic and international printing), the cost advantages and supply chain advantages you get when producing domestically in the USA, and the disadvantages with exporting or importing business from overseas. This trip was a trip that fast-forwarded my learning curve and transitioned me to master magician. I had earned my stripes by going undercover, and I set my sights on continuing the same strategies here in the States. The next few months I spent cold-calling and winning business by merely talking above my competition. I quickly realized that what I was up against in this market were a bunch of uneducated sales reps that were told by their upper management to go sell this new packaging segment called "Flexible Packaging."

You see, what I realized was the niche segment of the printing industry that I was positioned in was what old-timers would call the "label industry." Label printers were print companies with 7 in., 10 in., or maybe 13 in. wide printing presses and that had been around for decades. The label industry is what it sounds like. These were printers that printed stickers that went on jars. These were businesses built by "gray hairs" with no innovation. These businesses were often family owned and passed down to the sons or the next generation. By default, flexible packaging films could be printed on these printing presses, but that does not qualify these label companies to do so. In the '90s these films started to become readily available to label companies, and by default these label companies started printing on them without doing proper research or being qualified. The presses running sticker material did not have the tension controls needed to print unsupported films for flexible packaging and the quality in the market suffered due to this. You want to know how or why cancer keeps getting worse and came out of nowhere? Look at who regulates your packaging for the food you put in your body. NO ONE! Until the '90s the only companies truly using flexible packaging were Fortune 100 companies like Frito Lay, Pepsi, Proctor and Gamble, and other large firms.

Remember going into a grocery store and seeing a bag of beef jerky with a sticker on the outside of the ziplock bag? That type of packaging was the only option a small brand had for their packaging. Thus, they would buy bulk blank bags and then have a label converter print a sticker to go on the outside of the premade bag.

You see, that trip to China gave me a leg up on the "sticker printers" of America. Although label companies knew where to obtain these films and structures to print chip bags, they did not understand why they were using those structures. They didn't understand the interaction of the oils from the chips and the sealant layers of the film. I immediately looked at all the label companies dabbling in this flexible packaging market and saw that only a few had printing presses with widths wider than 13 inches and most did not have presses capable of controlling the tensions.

So how would that small brand ever get packaging that looked as professional as the big brands? How would they stop slapping stickers on premade stand-up bags and start getting the stand-up bag custom printed? How would they get clean printed goods out of a facility meeting or exceeding FDA regulations? Me!

The next size of press was typically 16 or 18 inches, and in the label industry that was considered wide web! I went on an espionage trip all over the USA in a rented Chevy Cobalt with no power steering and no cruise control. I acted as if I was a customer with a brand that needed printing, and just like the overseas printers they let me right in. I saw what they were working with in their production facility.

I saw what brands they printed for and what types of flexible packaging they were into. I saw how they stored their press equipment, who supplied their raw materials, and how they positioned the flow of their facility, and I saw machines doing things I did not know my press could do. Once I returned from that trip, I called machine manufacturers and asked technical questions about how to get my press to autoregister jobs, I called suppliers I saw in those facilities to get raw material pricing, and I reorganized the flow of our facility. I then separated my brand's reputation by doing several things that addressed market weaknesses. First, I marketed our company as the only "DIRECT FOOD CONTACT PRINTER" in America. No one else was doing this! This was genius. I was not lumped into the label (sticker) printer market, and I was developing a new category for printing.

Think about it. A customer calls and says they have a quote from TVC label (a sticker printer in north Dallas) and would like me to give them a competitive quote for some food grade flexible packaging. I then say, "Oh, TVC? Well, they are a label company and I am a 'Direct Product Contact printer.' The quote will not be apple to apples due to our facility standards, print methods, and ingredients. I would educate the consumer with facts about Label Companies and how they had been around forever and how neither their equipment nor their facility was suited for flexible package printing. Flexible Packaging is any packaging that is not hard and bends slightly while still holding a shape. It can be a pouch with a zipper (such as a bag of shredded cheese), envelope or pouch (such as your chili seasoning mix, Splenda packet, Swiss Miss cocoa pouch), granola bar wrapper, candy wrapper, chip bag, sample packet of shampoo you get in a magazine, etc. Do you understand? Its flexible delivery systems for products to get to a consumer. It is packaging where the contents of the package are touching the inside of the film? "DIRECT PRODUCT CONTACT." It can be the lidding film on your yogurt cup, etc. These are the films and products we were going after to print. Gone were the days that people wanted boxes and big plastic tubs. People wanted convenience, single-serving portions, etc.

I would explain the things the customer should look for in a vendor for food packaging, and I 100 percent won over every bid as I came across as more knowledgeable. I never lost. Were my competitor's facilities up to par with industry standard? Sure/maybe. Were my competitors using the right inks? Probably. Weren't the other sales reps doing this decade's longer than I was? Yup! Was my steel barn sufficient for a food grade facility? NOPE. However, the audience only sees what you let them see. This is a Sleight of Hand!

This sales tactic is called selling by instilling fear in the consumer, and it is used by the biggest and best companies. Even if the customer went back to the label printer and asked them questions to validate if I was telling the truth or not, the sales reps for those companies were clueless. They often conceded the loss and said yeah, "We are primarily a label printer." I later learned from a customer in Dallas that a couple of the label printers around Dallas discontinued the offering of flexible packaging "due to this young punk up in north Dallas selling stuff below market value." Hilarious! I was putting label companies out of business, as labels were on the decline and flexible packaging was the vehicle you were going to need to sell for the future. I dug deep into the soil and planted our roots as this specialty printer with there really being no difference between my actual process and any Label converters, process. It was a niche way of presenting my brand to the market and I performed it beautifully. Again, it was about framing! This was my angle. This was my epiphany! This was how I would separate myself from being just another magician. How will you separate yourself from your competitors? How will you sustain it? This is how I become a generational icon in a century-old industry. This in business terms is called how you become a market disrupter.

Every great entrepreneur or magician has an element of originality to their story, and this was mine. I realized I was competing with amateurs in something I knew more than they did about. This fueled me to stay ahead of my sector of the industry in knowledge, and it guided me on where to steer my efforts for innovation. Many times my common sense proved wrong the best and highest paid engineers in our industry. The billion-dollar brands in our industry were baffled when I proved theories wrong, but it happened several times. For decades, certain films were not used for certain industries due to case studies from the '80s or '90s. Several times, major corporations steered away from using a certain film due to a failure in the market, but my lack of industry knowledge became a benefit. Because I did not know any better, I tried things that engineers would not have tried due to case studies they were privileged to in school. I disproved theories about OPP films melting in heat sealable applications, and I designed my own line of products that gave me a competitive advantage.

And every chance I had, I spit out the words "Direct Product Contact Printer." I was the only one calling myself that. I coined that phrase and it follows my brand to this day. As we grew, I would recite stats that grew with our brand. You may or may not remember McDonald's back in the day and the tagline under their sign? It said "MILLIONS SERVED DAILY" and then years later they changed it to "BILLIONS SERVED DAILY." It was a subtle change to every sign across America, and one they didn't advertise they made, but they made it. I would say, "Over 10 million packets produced and no failures in the market!" I would change it year after year, subtly, and now I state, "Over billions of packets served and no failures in the market!" That means no leakers, no delamination, no bad product getting to the consumer in an unintended manner! Your word choice and the discrete way you evolve your brand's image are both a matter of shell games. Who can track back that stat? No one, but it's a tagline similar to what McDonald's used, and taglines work!

Nearly a year in business and still being in the red, I continued on. So long as the cash flow was there, I continued on. I was not profitable, but the cash flow was there to play the ball under the cup game with vendors. I may have pissed off some vendors by slow paying them, but if the funds were there, I continued to put on a show.

After eight months of being in business, I pitched to my old business partner to come join the printing company as a third partner. He had no experience either, but he was a smart and well-grounded mind who could help me navigate the choppy waters ahead. He was the ideal stagehand. Plus, if I failed, it would have been nice to fail with someone else than be all by myself!

8

♠

Reality Distortion

In my story I started out as a small party magician, but I immediately named myself the CEO. Does a two-person operation have a CEO? I saw myself through a reality distortion filter. This filter is an essential tool for every entrepreneur, as it convinces even you that you are who you say you are. Obviously a startup company CEO is a joke compared to those guys on Wall Street, but I was a CEO, wasn't I? Sure, I cleaned the toilets, ran machines, managed the sales, and was one of only three employees, but I was the CEO! Since I was a CEO, I acted like a CEO. I talked like a CEO and I bought an Audi A4 so that I looked like a CEO. I could not even afford the interest on that car, but my vision as a magician was the Vegas strip, and birthday parties were a part-time gig for me. I never let my customers know I was performing birthday parties (an analogy for printing for small brands or barely surviving with enough business to keep the lights on).

In reality, I did not own one suit or tie, but I had the car, I had the title, and I began putting on an illusion. I convinced myself that I was this big-time executive, which encouraged me to keep playing the part, much like I convinced myself I was like those kids on reality TV when I was in Colorado in order to get my confidence back; my ability to distort reality was key. I remember how empowering it felt to call vendors and potential customers and say, "Yes, this is the CEO of ABC Co. and I would like to speak to your CEO please!" There is so much more power in that than calling up as a nobody solicitor or salesman.

I believed my illusion regardless of how far away from reality it was. I went straight to the decision-maker on every sales call instead of targeting the purchasing manager. Funny thing:

TRICK #4: Purchasing Managers will do business with whomever their boss tells them to.

Think about it. Often the person who makes the decisions can be influenced by the person who writes their paycheck!

I knew it was only a matter of time before I became who I wanted to be, so I just lived a split life: one that put on the show of the future and one that built the present day brick by brick. It was never difficult for me to put on this act, as I was a natural performer anywhere I could get an audience.

As an entrepreneur building a business, you'll face plenty of rejection. Who wants to bet on a new startup with no history of success and zero track record? Would you hire a magician for your five-year old's birthday party with zero reviews on Yelp? Would you let a surgeon operate on you if you knew it was his first surgery out of med school? Bill Gates knew this when he took orders for his first computers that he had not even fully designed yet and then built them in his garage! He performed well enough to convince someone for an opportunity and then went behind the curtain to do what he had to for that first order. He had no product to offer, but he had sold his customers as if he did, and they bit on the illusion.

People only know what you allow them to see and hear.

People saw me as a CEO. People **assumed** I had a large production facility. People **assumed** I was 50 plus employees, but why? Did they make those things up, or did I plant those illusions in their mind? They probably assumed these things as I told them highlights. No one has time these days to hear the whole story, so get really good at narrowing it all down to the highlights. I told people we had expansions going on back at the facility, but did we? What did that mean? Was it just a ploy, or maybe we were adding a women's bathroom, as we only had a men's bathroom in the beginning. What they assumed expansion to mean was up to them. I told them that we were several thousand square feet and that we ran 24/7. (Guess what? Today we are and today we do!) Back then we were 8,000 sq. ft, and technically I lived in that barn, so we were always open. Does that count as a 24/7 operation? Maybe that was a harmless white lie.

Imagine what the customers thought and the credibility any business has that is operating around the clock. Operating around the clock means we have processes in place, it means we are in high demand, it means we are healthy; or does it? No, we weren't making money around the clock, but I sure as hell was washing pans or working 24 hours a day hustling for the next deal. To me that justified telling people we were 24/7, plus I knew the sophistication a manufacturing facility has to have in order to operate 24/7. I used that line as leverage to gain credibility and to make us appear in high demand. At the end of the day, all you care about is if they believe the illusion. It's also not a lie if you truly believe it to be true or if you believe it will become a truth in the near future. This was simply business.

You are who you say you are, **but don't lie to yourself.**

From this information these people formed their own opinion of who I was and what that CEO title meant for me. So what kind of entrepreneur are you? What gigs do you want as the magician? Could you frame your audience better than you are doing currently? Could you tease and lead your audience to make assumptions more? Don't share more than you have to. Are you a local magician or one who aspires worldwide fame? Stories sell. What's yours?

Make yourself interesting. Be original in everything you do; and be confident. As I met with prospect after prospect, name-dropping Fortune 100 brands, it was rare for someone to ask to see our facility, as they assumed that if companies of that stature were doing business with us, then it had to be legit. I had worked with Abbott and I would use that time and time again.

I would tell the customer that I was looking for cornerstone brands to build a printing empire with. I emphasized how good my relationship was with Abbott, why they choose to work with us as a cornerstone, and the trial runs we had going for Nestle and Kellogg's. The trial run statement was false, my relationship with Abbott was not amazing by any stretch, but the fact that Abbott was ordering from me gave me clout.

You hear Abbott and you think health and wellness.

You hear Abbott and you think pharmaceutical. I knew that, and when I dropped Abbott's name in a sales call, the next thing I would emphasis was that we were not just another label printer. We are a "Direct Product Contact Printer." All of our ingredients are FDA compliant and only a small percentage of printers in America meet those standards. Again, NO WAY TO FACT-CHECK THIS.

Did we print for any other Fortune 100 brands at the

time? Maybe, but I name-dropped several to gain confidence. The smoke and mirrors made it seem as if we had about 50 employees. I would even show print samples that we did not print, but that I was given on my travels around the world. I never claimed to print those samples, but those samples were intended to represent the type of packaging and printing we could offer. Business is all about the "fine print." Why do you think the fine print is so small? The commercials or advertisements want you to assume it's a good deal! It's never as good of a deal as it seems once you read the fine print! Business is all about assumptions. If people assumed we printed those samples, that was on them. In reality there were about three to four of us employed by the company, and we had no brag book of print samples to show of our own because we only had a customer or two. I even disguised my voice when answering calls to make it seem that we were bigger than we were.

When people called for me, I would respond as the receptionist, "Hold on one moment and I will see if he's available," I said. "Sorry, but he is in a board meeting," or "Let me check his office," or "He is on the production floor holding a quality meeting." What? Where did that come from? We didn't have a board. I didn't host any meetings. It was a Sleight of Hand trick I used to make our company seem larger. At times I had my girlfriend pose as a receptionist and had friends run local deliveries to customers, posing as employees just so local customers would associate more faces with the brand.

The more faces the customers saw representing the brand, the bigger they assumed I was. I have since then spoken to many successful entrepreneurs who have used these same techniques, having their wives pose as receptionists when inviting people in to tour the facility. Little things like that can make or break a deal. It is all about the smoke and mirrors.

My wife still says I owe her for the times she posed as an

employee or delivered product to a customer as an assistant. My wife claims I owe her a royalty for the message she recorded on my cell phone back then. What important person records their own voicemail? I believe back then it was my wife's voice saying, "Thank you for reaching out to Dru Riess. He is extremely busy, but anxious to return your call. Please leave your name, number, and reason for the call and he will be sure to get you on his calendar to respond to as soon as possible."

I call it Sleight of Hand, and in 1987 Donald Trump called it a truthful hyperbole. A hyperbole on its own is an exaggerated statement or claim not meant to be taken literally. The truth part of this is getting people to believe what you believe is true even though it may not be.

When the Trump Tower was built, he lied about how many floors there really were in order to sell the higher floors at a premium. Call him a liar, be upset, or get on board. Business has always been done like this. Who did he hurt with that white lie? What did he gain?

The truthful hyperbole was my most used technique.

A **truthful hyperbole** is something you think is real because it feels real to you. Even though it's exaggerated, you believe it to be real. People would ask, "How large is your facility where you print?" Again, I would say, "We are several thousand square feet." Don't ever say you're in an 8,000 sq. ft. steel shed off a gravel road. Saying "several thousand square foot" lets the customer fill in the blank. I believed it to be an honest answer, and it made me feel at ease answering the question that way. I spoke with a pace and went on to the next subject quickly after answering any question like that.

The best day of your life is the day that you yourself see the truth, and that others see you as what you have been performing as. The day you walk into your vision and you

become what you have been performing as is the moment the magician walks into his prestige.

Despite all of the unattractive things that surrounded my company that I was building, my eyes had **distortion goggles** on them. We had rats, snakes, and crickets all over the facility. We had huge deer that would come sit right by our entry door to the barn, we had bobcats that would stroll on by the open dock door of the barn in broad daylight, and once we had a wild boar try to break down the front door at 1:00 a.m. by pounding his head into the door, trying to get into the facility.

We had raccoons that would get stuck in our trash cans and coyotes that roamed around our facility at dusk. It was pitch dark and it was scary, but it was what I was given to work with. In my eyes, I saw what it would become in two, five, ten years, not what it was then. I could have been holding a crystal ball with the vision I had, because it's a reality today.

Way back before it was a reality, I saw a food grade facility with GMP and FDA certifications, I saw Segways zipping around a larger and more state-of-the-art facility, I saw several printing presses not just one, and I saw the latest technologies. It was in my imagination, but also in my heart to believe it would come true.

I saw a wall in our main lobby that would have colored water flowing down it as symbolism for the ink that runs through our veins, and I saw us on the cover of all the industry trade magazines. I saw it so clear, which made it that much easier to navigate toward.

Like a chef in the kitchen of your favorite restaurant, the customer only cares about what the end product tastes like. You don't think there are mistakes that happen in even the nicest restaurants? Of course, there are still fires in even the best kitchens, but you must only show the customer what you want them to see and taste. How believable you are in selling your vision depends on how much you believe in your vision yourself. Get into character and your performance will be more believable.

Everyone knows magic is fake, but how much you believe in your illusion is how much your audience will believe it.

If you're an entrepreneur, you are bound to be hated at some point. You will get judged, talked about, and criticized by others, but understand that you choose who and what you let influence your efforts. That's the life of an entrepreneur: always trying to gain others' approval and trying to prove your ideas are worthy. If you act like you already have validation for your ideas and that you have already proven yourself, others will buy into that as well.

I was hustling, and I was getting opportunities. I did try and run the cleanest facility in the country, and we did keep up with FDA regulations, but we were by no means certified by a third party or validated as one of the only "Direct Product Contact Printers" in America. I hope by now you understand there really was no such thing.

Compared to our competitor we had the same equipment, same capabilities if not less, but we made you feel better about choosing us for your "Direct Product Contact Printing" because we angled it as our specialty. The customer heard what I needed them to hear in order to **give us an opportunity, and that's all anyone can ever ask for in business.**

9

♠

Sleight of Hand is the Foundation for all Business

If for one second, you are judging me right now, stop! You cannot judge me for being aware of what the market needs and how to get around it or do what needs to be done because at some point you'll have to do it too. Being an entrepreneur is a juggling act. It's a constant give-and-take, and it brings out the best in you, the warrior in you, and the fighter in you.

Some people knew about our facility. I could not keep them all away, but those who came out saw something in me. Some people turned a blind eye and asked me to hurry and pull this off before their bosses found out. Some of those brands are brands you have purchased, and all business is done like this. You work with people you like, plain and simple. Think of the relationships in your own life. You go the extra mile for people you like and believe in, so make sure you are passionate about what you do.

I was confident in myself, but their confidence and belief bought me time—and time makes profits; profits allow progress, and when you're committed to reinvesting it all back into the growth of your business, it's a bonus. This is the guts of the book. This is Business 101! Pay attention here and have an open mind. While reading this chapter, begin to relate to your situation, your business, how you could slightly change the way you present something, and how you can get more business. You may have to work harder than you thought, and that's okay. You may have to make a presentation that talks to your vision and not where you are today, and that's okay too. Bill Gates did it when he didn't even have a software system to sell, but convinced IBM to partner with him. He sold the vision, and then he delivered on it.

Think about the way companies advertise today.

When Chevy advertises, they have the most JD Power & Associate awards of any other American car manufacturer. Who the hell knows what that means? What is JD Power? Your everyday American has no idea what the credentials are for the award, and most of those awards are awards you have to pay for. Did you know that? Chevy's marketing team pays top dollar to gain these nonsense awards, as this is their top element of SMOKE.

Ford does not waste as many resources on the JD Power award platform. Sure, they, too, probably buy a few, but their advertising says, "Best-selling truck forty years in a row!" What average consumer can fact-check that? How are they the best-selling truck if they didn't win as many awards? Who actually verifies that fact if Chevy is the JD Power award leader the past four years? What matters more: sales or accolades? Sales! Accolades are a form of smoke and mirrors to trick a transaction into happening. Both of these companies use the most positive statistic they can scrape together in order to manipulate a car buyer to choose them over the competition. In most cases, they exaggerated the way a hyperbole should be exaggerated. In some cases, they may make these stats up because there is no way to fact-check it. This is all Sleight of Hand manipulation. All successful businesses make up stats to lure their audience in. Don't you remember a government bailout for GM and Ford that cost the taxpayers $80 billion? How are you the best-selling vehicle when you're bankrupt and get bailed out? How good are you at business if your business fails and you use loopholes to keep your company afloat? That's like bragging about winning the NIT tournament. That means you're the best of the losers. Don't we remember the city of Detroit nearly imploding? If you want to sell, you have to sell the positives. Only show what you want people to see and hear. How many times must I say this? It's not corrupt—it is business. **You have to be in business to stay in business**; thus, loopholes are there to give you a second, third, or fourth chance. Now stop and soak that line in as you will need to pull this line out several times while facing tough decisions. **YOU HAVE TO BE IN BUSINESS TO STAY IN BUSINESS.**

Can a company exist for 100 years as a breakeven company? Yes. So long as your expenses are paid and money is not being lost, you're still in business. That's like being tied at the end of 14 innings of a baseball game! No one has won, but no one has lost yet. As a business owner, you have to be in business to have a shot at the next inning. You have to be in business! No one can sustain a business losing money year after year. Do what you must, make tough decisions, and remember, YOU HAVE TO BE IN BUSINESS TO STAY IN BUSINESS. Do what you must to give yourself more time as you figure out how your trick will end. Buy yourself time and make sure you at least break even!

If you're about to graduate college, or if you're about to start your own business, you better be okay with everything I am mentioning. Think about bankruptcy and why it exists. It's a Get Out of Jail Free card, and there are different tiers of it available catered to keep the rich, rich and the poor, poor. Rich people file for bankruptcy to protect their wealth. The poor file bankruptcy that suppresses them for the rest of their life. What judge or group of people thought this up centuries ago? What was their motive? Surely there was a monetary gain for someone, and you can bet there was a kickback at the legislative level when bankruptcy became a thing in the late 1700s. **In other countries, if you don't pay a debt, you lose a limb or even your life.** Here in America the show must go on, and the rich must be given second chances when they fail. This is why bankruptcy exists! This is how GM is still here to interrupt your Sunday afternoon football game with deceiving commercials and a plethora of fine print at the bottom of the screen.

Business is dirty, and it is dog-eat-dog or you will get eaten. No one can be trusted. Those who have a fish symbol on the back of their car are the most corrupt, and you need to be able to navigate around the really bad people in the world. It has always been and always will be this way. Sell the business and then live up to their expectations. Deliver more than you promised and they'll be glad they bought from you. It's as simple as that, but how do you gain the opportunity? Once you have the opportunity, is it a straight transaction or is there a Sleight of Hand trick involved?

I built my dream home in 2015 for a million dollars. In 2018 I realized I had mold in my master bath shower. I hired a tile specialist to come in and assess the damage. The tile specialist informed me that my builder pulled a Sleight of Hand on me and never paid extra to have my tile sealed anywhere in my house. By then my two-year home warranty had expired and I had to pay out of pocket $7,000 to get tile sealed that should have been sealed when the house was built. Was I upset? Sure. But I should have thought about checking things like this. I know better now. You don't know what you don't know, and unfortunately being a homeowner was not something I had a ton of experience in. Thus, I promise with any property I buy in the future, I will do a ton of due diligence on things like this. You live and you learn, and you have to clap for the builder who was shifty and profited a little bit more off my ignorance.

I know one of the original scientists who formulated Centrum multivitamins for Pfizer. In conversations with this scientist, he admits the entire nutraceutical industry is a scam. He says, "The fact is that consumers don't want to pay for real health. It is almost like the audience demands to be deceived." In order to make a true multivitamin with ingredients that work, the consumer would have to be willing to pay top dollar. This scientist told me when you go to Walgreens and look for vitamin C, there is more than one reason prices differ across brands. Indeed there are brands that spend more on marketing, those that have higher overhead, and some brands that are just greedy. Those brands are the ones that price their product at a higher price, use inexpensive packaging, and are trying to truly pull the wool over your eyes. However, they know they are not offering a superior product. The other reason certain brands may cost more is because the product costs twice as much to make. It cost more to make because it's the real deal. My friend Dr. Ross tells me that 70 percent of the products on the shelves today are placebos. When there is one brand of vitamin C being sold at $2 and one at $15, the most concerning thing is that consumers tend to go for the less expensive option immediately. Did you know nearly 90 percent of all vitamin C in the States has been sourced from China. There are no rules to regulate this and thus you never know the country of origin for the ingredients. Do you trust that 100 percent of what comes from China is pure and clean? Don't you believe those Chinese companies would pull a sleight of hand to gain a few more points of profit? Would they put fillers in the product to prosper? In fact, if we test most vitamin C in the market, you are likely consuming a supplement with GMOs. When you see ascorbic acid as an ingredient in your vitamin C, you are consuming synthetic vitamin C. On the back of the brand Nature's Made, their Vitamin C ingredient deck reads as is: "OTHER INGREDIENTS: Cellulose Gel, Hypromellose, Croscarmellose Sodium, Stearic Acid, Magnesium Stearate, Silicon Dioxide, Polyethylene Glycol." *I apologize if I misspelled any of those ingredients, as spell check could not even identify them as real words!* One question where is the Vitamin C? Most consumers see the ingredient deck and see both that say 1000 mg of vitamin C, but what else is in the bottle? Buy the bottle with less ingredients and more of what you actually want! Dr. Ross tells me that some of the products are ineffective due to the fillers added, lower grades of vitamin C, etc.

Dr. Ross is often asked to formulate and make supplement products for the consumer market. He is one of maybe 20 true scientists who do things right in the nutraceutical world, as he is a dinosaur in the industry. His career began with Pfizer and has continued into the nutraceutical world for decades. When he formulates a product and gives the formulation to a brand, the brand then goes and finds a "contract packager" that can produce the product in bulk and package it in an ideal delivery system.

A contract packager is a company that packages and sometimes produces a product from scratch for a brand that owns the formula. The brand that owns the formula may dual-source and have several co-packers across the country, or they may jump from co-packer to co-packer year to year for cost savings. Some contract packagers specialize in packing in one type of delivery system, such as stick packs, boxes, tubs, jars, or bottles, and others do multiple delivery systems under their roof. I hope you understand there are not several companies in the country that make shampoo, granola bars, dietary supplements, etc. There are contract packagers that specialize in producing one or a couple of these product lines. From there the big brands, such as P&G, Abbott, Alacer, Kellogg's, and Hormel, use the same contract packagers. A contract packager in Los Angeles blends and fills Herbal Life protein powders on one machine, the machine next to it is blending and filling Kashi, the next machine is filling Nutrisystem, and so on. Abbott or Kellogg's are simply the magicians. They really don't do anything but fund the business and direct the business from a macro level. All the true manufacturing and production of their goods are done by independent contract packagers. Does this make sense?

Head and Shoulders, Vidal Sassoon, and others do not all have their own facilities where they make shampoo. There are three or four contract packagers across the country that specialize in this. The P&Gs of the world are simply the magician while the stagehand does all the work. Considering that the actual production of the products is not done under the actual brand's own roof, do you think the contract packagers have their own agenda? Would you put it past a contract packager to substitute an ingredient in a granola bar, shampoo, or protein powder formula if it meant bigger margins for their company? You better not put it past them, as this happens daily. If you take products off the shelf and have an independent study done on them, you will find an alarming number of products that do not meet label claim. Perhaps the ingredients they say are in their product are in there, but then you have to wonder if the percentage of the claim is accurate, or if there are fillers added to meet the fill weights. Again, all businesses never show all their cards, and unfortunately the less control a brand has on their product, the larger the window for Sleight of Hand tricks to be done; and they are done!

The problem is that no one regulates that the original formula the scientist designed to truly benefit human health is what gets mass produced and put into the consumer market. What typically happens is that a "contract packager" takes the scientist's formula and sources all the raw materials based on volumes of projected sales by the brand. They then tell the brand that owns the formula that it will cost let's say $5 per unit to produce the exact formula designed by the scientist. The brand pushes back, as they cannot make a profit on that high of a cost; the market will only allow them to sell the product for $8 retail. Somewhere in there, they have to make a profit, their distributor needs to make a profit, and the retailer needs to make a profit. The "contract packager" then goes back and looks for ingredients that can be substituted with a different component and drive costs down.

By the time the product makes it to market, it is a shell of what the original formula was by the scientist and there are no clinical trials for the new cheaply sourced product. Thus, a placebo is introduced into the market but marketed with the results of what the original formula would have done. Is this not a SLEIGHT OF HAND? Is this not unethical? Who is the unethical one here? The "contract packager" for knowingly twisting and altering a scientist's proven formula to the point where it is not effective? The brand for allowing the product to be altered and still selling it to the market? Doesn't the brand care that they have substituted quality for cost? No! They don't. Because behind every brand name are people who have their own families to support and have their own agenda for success. The contract packager employees like being employed, and in order to be employed, they have to be in business. In order to be in business, the business owner has to get something in return, such as return on investments. If it comes down to the quality of an outside brand or your own company's survival, you will save your own company. It's the same as the age-old question, "Who would you die for?" The answer is likely to be your family first before you die for a random person; and you can only die once!

The bottom line is that 70 percent of the products on the store shelves are crap. I know for a fact. I have been in and out of hundreds of food packaging facilities, none of which look alike. Every company cares only about their bottom line, and some who say they are AIB certified, ISO certified, NSF certified, GMP certified, etc. are only doing so as a marketing ploy. These companies don't have a clue what it means to be certified, but put up a smoke-and-mirrors act for the auditors to gain the certifications. The certifications allow "contract packagers" to fool other brands to bring their products to them for mass production, and the circle continues. I have stood next to a guy eating a cheeseburger in a room where multivitamin pills were being filled! I was drinking a slushy standing next to him!

If you want to watch a cool video, look up a brand called Ritual. Ritual is a clean multivitamin brand for women that sources raw materials from better places than China. Ritual takes out a ton of bogus ingredients and compounds only the nine essential ingredients a woman's body actually needs. The vitamin is $30, but understandably so. When you look at Walgreens, Walmart, Amazon, etc. for a comparable product, a multivitamin for woman can range from $5 per bottle to

DRU T. RIESS II

$40 per bottle. After you watch this video about Ritual, you tell me that $5 bottle is just as good. I can assure you the $40 bottle on the store shelf is due to money spent in marketing, the packaging costs being higher due to their look on the shelf, or a greedy executive team that uses price to sway consumer confidence. You tell me where you think those raw ingredients are sourced and what the spectrum of price variance means to the quality of the product. Wake up! This is real. This is business.

Let's take it one step further. Let's not buy into Ritual's claim that they source from places other than China. I can guarantee if I went to Ritual's headquarters, they are not compounding their pills on site. I would bet anything they are outsourcing the pill manufacturing to a contract packager. What do you think the odds are that the contract packager originally sourced expensive ingredients from unique areas of the world and had Ritual sign off and believe their product was better? Then behind the curtain Ritual goes out and creates a great story and convincing video, then begins growing their business. However, behind the curtain either immediately, six months down the road, or possibly a year down the road, as the brand grows, the contract packager does a "switcharoo" behind the curtain. Instead of a more expensive omega-3 sourced out of Italy, the contract packager slips in the omega-3s they are buying in bulk from China at a huge discount, thus broadening the contract packagers bottom line, changing Ritual's approved formula, and the show goes on. You can't possibly taste an omega-3 change in the formula, and Ritual accepts some falsified COA documents as a valid means of confidence for their products quality. I hate to break it to you Ritual, but you too have been fooled by the magician. The only way to promise a consumer something or make sure something is done is to produce it yourself and have complete control. Look for the brands that truly manufacture their own good, but then vet out the leadership and investors behind that brand to find out what their agenda is.

Here are some other examples of normal Sleight of Hand tricks.

Car Rentals

I recently went to rent a car on my Kayak app. I was landing at LAX in a couple hours and needed a vehicle. I selected a premium vehicle from Enterprise. Under the picture of a Mercedes sedan, there was fine print that read "Chevy Impala or similar." I immediately realized this was a corporate Sleight of Hand. If Enterprise knows the best car I would get to choose from would be a Chevy, then why show me a Mercedes picture when I selected the premium option? Mercedes was not even a brand possible for me to receive, but an average consumer does not read the fine print and only sees the Mercedes and picks it due to the possibility of getting a Mercedes to drive for the day. When I arrived, I was given a Nissan Altima! Same thing, right? Wasn't this a Sleight of Hand? If business was honest, there would be no such thing as the "fine print."

Real Estate

When a Realtor sells a house and calls your Realtor, claiming they have a multiple bid situation, but they don't, is this a Sleight of Hand or just business? The Realtor knows you are the only offer, and even if you offer the seller's asking price, this is business. The seller's Realtor is squeezing you for more, and you likely go up a few thousand dollars. Again, this is business. Should Realtors be deemed as corrupt? Are they labeled as liars, or do people accept their role in their performance for what it is? Do you accept them for who they are and what they do as magicians?

Cheap Fish

Do you like sushi? How often do you eat it? I bet you eat it far less than you actually think. Remember the days when sushi was a Japanese delicacy? It wasn't long ago when sushi was not something served in grocery stores or on the menu at every neighborhood restaurant. There is a reason for that. A study done a few years ago proved that over 94 percent of the sushi served in America is not actually sushi. Every time you order a spicy tuna roll, California roll, or a sushi roll where the fish is chopped up, you are almost always eating a cheaper and more available substitution fish. In most cases, it isn't even fish at all. The study goes on to explain the dangers of eating this substitute fish, and no one regulates it. Why? Because it's profitable. Extremely profitable. When businesses are reaping huge rewards, legislation is slowed down. In most countries the sushi or fish market is highly regulated, but with all the loopholes in America, we make it acceptable. They claim if you must eat sushi in America, limit it to once a month, and if you must order raw fish, order whole pieces of fish. Whole pieces of fish are much harder to fake, and you're more likely to get real salmon or yellowtail by ordering nigari. Sleight of Hand or just business?

Clothing Brands

When you see a brand like a clothing line that says "Since 1892," doesn't it have a certain nostalgia to it? It shouldn't. That does not mean the clothing line has been around for over a century. Sometimes that just means that's when the family was established, not the brand. In other cases, the established dates are there to give the perception of a company that has been around for a long time, thus just a marketing ploy. Do you fact-check the established dates that brands claim? Should you?

For example, Abercrombie & Fitch was a company in 1892, but they were not the clothing company that existed in the 1990s and 2000s. In fact, Abercrombie & Fitch was a company in 1892 that sold fishing poles, boats, tents, outdoor goods, etc. Seriously? It gets better. Abercrombie & Fitch filed bankruptcy and closed its doors in 1976 until a Houston-based company resurrected the brand and bought the name of the company in 1978 and began selling clothing by mail order under the name. Is that the same company? No! Was it Abercrombie & Fitch that owned the company still, or was it just an entrepreneur/investor in Houston that used the name? Has Abercrombie & Fitch been around since 1892? Not really. This is a Sleight of Hand used to persuade consumers that this brand is timeless. In 1997 Abercrombie started popping up in every mall across America, targeting teenagers. In 1997 when I was in junior high, how cool would a sweatshirt be that said, "Abercrombie & Fitch Since 1997"? Not very cool, but people bought the brand and everyone bought the Sleight of Hand marketing ploy about this trendy company that had been around "Since 1892." None of it is true.

In today's market, where big label brands are not as appealing, it's crazy to see these new brands pop up and when they say they were established. It's a trick used often, and I suppose, use it if it works in your market. For me I could say my company was established in 2007, but why not say 1983. I was born in 1983, so I guess I could say the company was born when I was born. It's up to you, but don't be slighted by brands based on marketing ploys like this. Isn't this a truthful hyperbole? Whatever you think the reality is, you can put out there for your consumers to believe.

Retail Shelves

When you're shopping at the grocery store, do you think about the cost of shelf space? The brands that want to be placed at eye level pay a premium because statistically that is what consumers will see and grab before looking to the top or bottom shelves. All of this is manipulation and psychology used to gain business. Oftentimes the better brand for you is lower on the shelf, but those mom-and-pop brands that truly make their products with good ingredients cannot afford the shelf premium. The big label companies that mass produce products with preservatives, mass production runs, cheaper ingredients, and more get the sale due to having a bigger budget for marketing. Next time you're shopping, ask yourself how a certain product got placed on the end cap of the aisle. Look for the same product, but somewhere else on the shelf or in the store. Compare ingredients and compare pricing, and see if you're buying the best or just the product that the store gets a higher royalty for selling. Stores are motivated by kickbacks to sell more of certain products. Try to see the matrix and shop as an educated consumer and not one being manipulated by your surroundings. In fact, wear headphones and be talking to someone on the phone while shopping or put ear plugs in when shopping. Do not listen to the music, as retail stores subliminally play music to alter your decision-making. This is a very old trick, but it works. Next time you're shopping for clothes, listen to the music and realize that a highly paid marketing team has chosen what you are listening to due to research and how it alters someone's decision-making.

Fast Food

McDonald's sells McNuggets. Look out for anyone selling a nugget or a tender. Please note that chickens do not have nuggets or tenders as a physical feature on them. They have wings, thighs, legs, and breasts, but no nuggets. Please note that McDonald's still to this day has never said they serve CHICKEN nuggets, let alone chicken at all. Hell, Burger King is selling ten nuggets for $1.69. Who can do that if it's real meat? Why don't they call it real chicken? Because they can't. They claim pure white meat. What is that? That is the same thing I did. THE SAME! They slide past with vague answers and creative marketing. They say 100 percent pure white meat. Incubator-raised aliens? MSG-infused gum? How do we as consumers keep the magicians honest all around in every transaction, in every moment of life, or do we even care? Be aware of the details and the wording that corporations will use to lure you in. Use these tactics for your own gain if your line of work can benefit from it.

Misleading Claims about Mouthwash

Pfizer is a company worth nearly $200 billion and revenues per year of $50 billion or so. The company has 96,500 employees, yet how did they get there? Believe me, the biggest companies are the worst and most unethical because they can be. When Pfizer's brand of Listerine mouthwash claimed that using Listerine could replace flossing completely, do you think they knew that was a lie? Of course it was. Based on their own independent study under their own controlled environment, they said it had been tested. For years Pfizer reaped the reward of a growing brand in Listerine, and consumers were tricked. Not until 2005 did a judge deem this claim false and misleading. Pfizer was forced to pay millions and to pull ads that claimed the mouthwash could replace flossing completely. Do you think Pfizer cared? By then the penalty was paid for by profits from their corruption, and they still walked away with a brand that is on the store shelves today.

When companies do this and are found guilty, why isn't the brand put down completely? Why isn't their limb cut off? Oh yeah, the same reason we have bankruptcy in America. We are all about second chances and keeping the rich, rich. Are you telling me out of the 96,000 employees, these types of advertising tactics aren't approved by multiple committees and departments? Do you think Listerine is the only Pfizer brand that does this? Do you think Pfizer still pulls a million Sleight of Hand tricks per year? Because they do! It's business.

The same goes for brands such as Skechers and their Shape Up product line of shoes that you simply wear daily to replace the need for working out—a claim that was endorsed by a real chiropractor. But only later did you find out he was the husband of a Marketing Executive at Skechers. Again, a couple years after profiting mega profits, they were slapped on the wrist with a $40-million settlement, as there was no science behind their Sleight of Hand. However, by then $40 million was as a drop in the bucket compared to what they made while the program was running. Again, companies like Pepsi, Coke, Kellogg's, and others lose lawsuits every year due to unethical or Sleight of Hand marketing. Unfortunately, the reward is far greater than the penalty in business, so they will continue to do it and they will continue to prosper. Can you compete with this? The mega brands have the most to gain and losing only costs them a few pennies. You tell me that's not unethical. You tell me that's not a system set up for the big brands to stay on top.

In 2012 I bought a 32" press for $800,000 with no intention of turning it on. For starters the $800,000 was all the profit I had saved up for years, and I spent it all in order to give the essence of a more capable facility. Every time I gave tours of my facility, I worried what people thought, as I only had one press. I needed more than one press to pull of the façade of the revenues I was claiming I manufactured. I bought this machine to be a filler on my production floor. It was a conversation piece. To hook it up, pay for the learning curves of using it, and buy parts for it would have bankrupted my company back in 2012. I used it for what I needed it to be. It was bait. As I gave tours, people saw we were one of the only companies in the country that had a narrow web press (16" wide) and a wide web press (32") under the same roof. This gave me an advantage: this was a distraction in my left hand while I was doing something with my right. Soon I was printing $5,000,000 worth of business in wide web print, but I was doing it at a facility in Wisconsin. People never asked if I was printing their order at my facility. The customers saw the wide web press and assumed I was doing it in house, but I wasn't. It was not until 2015 that I fired that press up for the first time and started to pay for the learning curve involved with bringing a new asset online in a production facility. By 2016 I was producing 50 percent of the business I outsourced, and by 2018 I was no longer outsourcing anything. That is what I am talking about when I say you are who you believe you will become! Sometimes these tricks take years to develop, but if you know where you're going, you can navigate your viewers through until the end of the trick.

In 2011 when I first thought of buying my own 32" press, I immediately put a stock photo I found on the internet on our website. I put a picture of a beautiful brand-new wide web press on our website and made it look like it was in our facility.

I even had stock photos of what our facility looked like, and it helped gain credibility. I would receive calls asking about our company and saying it looked as if we had a world-class organization by the looks of the website. Your website is one of the most powerful smoke and mirror tools available to any business. Your website can be your first and last impression for a potential customer. Our website gave the feel that we had things others did not, and over the years as we actually looked the part, I strategically and quietly slipped real photos in place of the fake ones. By 2017 our facility looked exactly how I had described it would in 2007, and our equipment was even better than the stock photos I originally pulled a Sleight of Hand with.

Are you aware this is what business is? If all goes well and you perform well enough, **you must then be able to close your audience or your deal.** To repeat, ask for the opportunities. People won't just give you an opportunity—ask for it! My go-to line was, "Let me prove to you that we are the perfect partner for your brand/company and that you are the perfect cornerstone piece to what we are building." Take away their risk or lower it as much as possible. "I have three Fortune 100 companies I print for right now, and we are looking for that fourth cornerstone to secure our foundation as an industry leader."

In reality, we may have had no customers, or years later we had over 100 customers, but I never changed the wording. If we had a hundred customers, I wanted that next pitch to feel they would be a top four priority of mine. If we had only one customer, I wanted them to feel a top four priority of mine. The customer will be flattered when you see them as a possible cornerstone.

Customers want to know that they are not your guinea pig. Telling them they will be the final cornerstone makes them feel secure in their decision to give you an opportunity. It's a win-win! You must be able to wrap up the Sleight of Hand trick by closing your sales call! Selling isn't for everyone, and if it's not for you, you should reconsider being an entrepreneur. Be able to pop the question, "So do we have a deal?" But instead of calling it a deal, call it an opportunity. "So can I have an opportunity? Or what can I do for an opportunity? I'm so hungry to show you this is a win-win!"

Being creative can be the sustaining factor to a business that lasts. Are you willing to be open to new opportunities and revenue streams that might boost your existing offerings?

However, while being wily or using smoke and mirror tactics, I never plagiarized a document or falsified the quality of a product. Everything we did was done the right way, but maybe not in the facility or the type of facility I was hinting at in the beginning. The smoke and mirrors was just a distraction to the real trick. The truth in my game was that I was coming into this industry to revolutionize it and take it over; but I had to buy myself some time.

I love causing paradigm shifts. I love combating normal thought processes and behaviors. I love challenging the status quo.

I quickly realized this industry was trapped in a stagnant and traditional set of rules. Old-time business men were making huge margins, sales reps were reaping massive commissions, sales reps were vacationing with their customers' families, several were getting under-the-table kickbacks, and there was no level playing field for packaging consumers because no one had exposed it for what it was. It was a greedy man's industry. The printing industry was all one massive brokerage game. Very few companies were doing the actual manufacturing, and those that produced products were in it for the overhead margins, not for the security of their customers.

None of the existing brands were relevant to this new generation. The brands around were purely the aftermath of the baby boomer generation. Grandfathers and fathers passed on their printing businesses in the '70s, '80s, and '90s to the next generation of family business owners.

Twenty years later, those guys kept their inheritance afloat with the same methodologies and practices that their predecessors built the business on: *You scratch my back, I scratch yours*; Fortune 100 companies are the only brands that matter; ignore the mom-and-pop-sized companies. However, there was a problem with that. No one was playing defense! The old retired "gray hairs" who once passed down their companies were now investors, and some of them were buying multiple print shops and merging them together as a conglomerate, but leaving their families in place to run and operate the mergers. Unfortunately, those family members were not entrepreneurs, and they often dropped the ball. No one was looking out for Generation X or the millennial generations that would follow and bring new insight into this stagnant business. In fact, it's not just the printing industry but rather a ton of older industries are awaiting the next market disrupter.

I came in like a tornado, uneducated with the way the industry was supposed to work, unaware of the margins and practices that were "normal." I was unfiltered, careless to the good old boy network that had built so many of these brands. I was the market disrupter this industry was **unprepared for.** My advice is to be the guy no one see's coming. Be the outside the box thinker, the dreamer, the guy asking why it has to be a certain way, and the one asking for the opportunity! When a company has been in business for 20 plus years, and they have clients who have been with them just as many years, they have to have some fear that something or someone is going to come along and bring change.

Most companies are about profit first and customers second. Their mission statements, their brand promises say otherwise, but they are BS. From day one I emphasized how I was all about the customer. I was all about capitalizing on any opportunity I was given.

I knew that one way to provide value was to treat the customer better. I knew another way was speed and consistency. *What can I give the customer that others are not giving? How can I service them in a way others are not?* I believed the law of averages played in my favor if only I took care of the customer like a friend and not a customer. I asked customers or potential customers what the headaches were in their purchasing position. Nine out of ten told me turnaround times are too slow in the film buying industry. Others said the pricing is confusing and they simply want to know what the invoice would look like after the job...because there were too many hidden costs.

So I asked myself, *How fast can I get this job done? How can I give clean and simple-to-read pricing? What factors are in my way of fulfilling a customer's order even faster next time? How can I make it for less and pass those savings on to the customer to gain more value in my relationships?* Wait...what? Did I just say that? Yes! *How can I make it for less and pass the savings on?* It wasn't about me. It wasn't about the short game. This was a long-term play. This was a marathon, and as an outsider trying to compete with bigger companies that had better technologies, more product lines, more fine print, more years being a magician, and more established contacts, what else did I have to offer but to expose the industry's weaknesses? I was more about setting myself up for continuous opportunities rather than squeezing the customer on that one transaction. At times I did things at cost to get the next opportunity; at times I did a job at a loss to squeeze my competitors out of all future opportunities. This was a trick I used often, but only if I truly believed it would work.

I knew that I could make every one of those weaknesses my company's strengths, and I gained all of the opportunities through some sort of Sleight of Hand trickery and my ability to come off as authentic. Was anything I did different than any other business? Wasn't I doing exactly what had to be done to compete and build a business? Would you have done something different? If you would have done something different, you wouldn't have made it!

10

Define What Your Ice Is

I have a friend who told me a story once about a thermos. I think that story is worth sharing with you and I want you to "define your ice." In 2016 his wife approached him and told him she was going to buy two Yeti cups when they were out shopping. The guy asked his wife, "How much are they?"

She replied, "Forty bucks."

He looked at her with that look husbands give when their wives say something that sounds bizarre. *"Forty bucks?"*

She said, "Each!"

"What?!" he exclaimed, then he realized this was a battle he would not win, so he smiled and said, "Okay, honey."

Later that night he filled his new cup up with ice and water and put it by his bedside. The next morning, he awoke to something he had never seen before. His cup of ice water still had ice filled to the rim of the cup. He smiled to himself and realized he didn't buy a cup—he bought the ice. The moral of this story is to ask yourself, What is my ice?

Realize that Yeti is not selling you a cup. Yeti is selling you what you desire.

In my business **my ice was my turnaround times.** My two-week turnaround promise is the ice the customer wanted, but doesn't know they want until they experience it. As we began consistently producing these rapid turn times, the word-of-mouth referrals were endless. This was game-changing to the industry and would have been to any business model in 2008 to 2014. Companies in these times cut back on spending, watched their spending, turned to JIT production and ordering methods, and managed inventory differently than they use to prior to the economy crashing in 2007.

Have you ever heard of Raising Cane's Chicken Fingers? Raising Cane's is a fast-food chain that specializes in fresh, never-frozen chicken tenders. Their menu is simple and their business model is one I copied. Unlike McDonald's, which offers everything from coffee, tea, mocha lattes, burgers, chicken sandwiches, sausage biscuits, burritos, pancakes, salads, and more, Raising Cane's only offers chicken fingers. If you want a sandwich, they put chicken fingers on two pieces of bread. Think about this business model and think of the inventory system's simplicity compared to what McDonald's requires.

I was the first to do this in food grade packaging! In essence, a customer would come to me and say, "I want this because my previous printer gave me this," and I would respond, "I'm sorry I do not offer that, but I do offer a product that looks and feels the same but performs better." I pushed my customers into one of five materials based on the aesthetic look they wanted in the market, the functionality they needed for the consumer's use, and the barrier properties the product itself required. In some cases, the structures I pushed clients into were overkill, but I could sell it to them for a competitive price due to the mass quantities I ordered it in. The result was my warehouse being very clean, very lean, and easy to manage.

This was market disrupting! This was another element of ICE!

As I was learning the industry and networked with people in the industry or retired from the industry, most people would be quick to tell me how they built their print company. Retired owners would tell me who they used for suppliers along with the history of how Avery Dennison Fasson and Mac Tac came about (the two conglomerate brokers of raw materials in the market at the time). I was curious so I would research these companies before building a relationship with them. During my research I looked into those companies and asked myself one thing, Are they a manufacturer or are they a broker?

Why did I want to know that? Because it changes the game. If they were brokers, then they were just marking the deals up and farming them out. If they were manufacturers, then they were actually handling the majority of their business and could get me raw materials faster. I wanted to know who was the real magician, and who was a pretender.

To my surprise, the two largest material suppliers to my segment of the market were brokers. **The two biggest suppliers in this industry were middle men!** This knowledge explained so many things. This slowed down the process to get answers from technical support when something went wrong with an order, fluffed up costs that didn't need to be there, and slowed deliveries to customers. I made my mind up that I would find out who the true manufacturers were in this industry, and I would build organic relationships—direct relationships.

I was committed to figure out how the magic trick was done. This was harder than I thought it would be, as the true manufacturers were $200 million to $2 billion extrusion businesses that had no interest in working with an $800k business operating out of a North Texas barn.

So how did I build relationships with these huge companies and immediately have my raw materials coming in 30 percent to 40 percent less than my competitors? How did I gain my third element of ICE? The short version of a long story is by utilizing a Sleight of Hand or "smoke and mirrors." Gossip. Distraction! When I had a call with a supplier, I held my cards close to the vest. I would plant small rumors about our Dallas facility being our first domestic facility, but that we had a division in Korea that had been printing internationally for years. (COMPLETELY FALSE). I would elaborate our goals to build our main location here in Dallas, and I would boast about new equipment to maximize our printing load that would be coming in to our shop that following year.

It was about creating the illusion of strategic and explosive growth. This tactic often leads to suppliers wanting to come visit the facility. I wasn't in the position to bring them to the barn and share the secrets of my tricks yet. Like a grand illusionist, I was always unavailable for a tour. "Sorry, we had auditors in" or "We had a customer from Europe visiting" (no, we didn't, but it sounds good). There was always a reason why a visit was impossible. All part of the grand magic trick.

TRICK #5: **Always talk about where you are going and not where you are, as I said before, but describe what your future as a company looks like and people will meet you there in their imagination.**

This tactic worked and it got me a direct relationship with the suppliers. It got me trial runs of material at a cheap price, and the rumors of our hypothetical growth and success spread like wildfire. Soon, I was visiting potential customers around the country, and upon meeting them they had already heard about us before. I was shocked! How? How would you have heard about a brand with now six employees and virtually no customers? Rumors! That's how.

I realized the manufacturers I told rumors to were gossiping about my company. The manufacturers and other printers were talking to each other, asking questions, and even talking to their other customers. Their curiosity was piqued about this up-and-coming company. Other Dallas printers were finding out about a new printing empire being built right in their backyard. Those printing companies around Dallas deployed their sales reps to find out more about this new company. I had ink vendors and machine part vendors and more being asked if they knew anything about this company that supposedly came out of nowhere and was backed by a huge Korean sister company.

Learning about the gossip gave me the chance I needed to really have fun with it. Every conversation I had with my ink vendor was a chance to drop a bit of information in his ear, a drop of sexy talk. It was like the game telephone. Whispering secrets to different people showed me who my true partners were and who the gossipers were. To one ink vendor I would tell them we grew last month by $1 million in revenue and we were looking at a new press to bring in sooner than later. Again, no, we weren't, but if that rumor got out, it would instill fear in my local competitors. I would tell another vendor some version of the truth, and to the next vendor I would tell them we were opening a Mountain Region Division and currently looking at facility space in Colorado or Utah. None of this was true! Then finally I would say we were going to build on a 50,000 sq. ft. addition to take on new capital expenditures. It was nuts!

When you give people the chance to take a story and run with it, you only need to give them bits of information. You can see the information transform into something different. Completely morphing your story into something fantastical.

The funny thing was, we began to hear feedback. I was once told I was "full of piss and vinegar"—whatever that means. We were four to five guys in a barn. We had a crappy old press, and we were talentless, but the façade was there. The façade had us busting at the seams with growth. The façade had us funded extremely well from our hypothetical international partners that did not exist, and we had more equipment and more employees month after month in this façade fairy tale. None of it was true, but it set our competitors on edge as the brand continued to grow.

Let people talk. The greatest part about these rumors is that it took me seconds to plant them, and then I never consumed another minute of my time with it. What my competitors did with this information was worry and exhaust resources combating what we were doing. They spent their time wondering how we were producing goods at the prices we were and how we were turning jobs in 48 hours.

How did we figure out the ICE in the industry and how did we design the business model to provide it? Again, the industry norm was four to six weeks. Later in the company's existence (2017) we started to offer stand-up bags with a three-week turnaround promise. The industry average for stand-up bags in 2018 was ten- to sixteen-week lead times. That is market disrupting; that is defining ICE! I didn't do it once or twice; rather, but four times I defined ICE in a century-old industry, and each time our business prospered from having these illusions mastered.

The competition wondered how we did it and who the hell we were. For at least the second time in this book: **"Mind your business!"**

Do not distract yourself with what your competitors are

doing and do not try to be like them! Oftentimes you will get sucked into a funnel of boredom chasing your competitors. Don't bore your audience!

What I didn't realize at the time was that while I was working hard to distinguish myself as different and create a new industry standard, these other companies were trying to be me. That was their biggest mistake. A good magician does not expose all the elements of the trick and never teaches how the trick is pulled off. A good magician disguises his movements so people cannot mimic them or follow a trail of bread crumbs. They should have known I was better than that! I was not going to make this easy for them to duplicate.

These shell games I played with my competitors distracted them from paying attention to their own business. They were too worried with what we were doing to be engaged in their own business, and I plucked brand by brand from them.

I never worried about twisting myself up or forgetting who I told what to. In the end, all the rumors were figments of my imagination, but they were a vivid depiction of what I was confident I would build. My vision was going to be real and became real every day I showed up to perform. It was just part of the process of building the grand illusion into a reality. **Believe it, and then you will see it.**

In the end these Sleight of Hand tricks led to me gaining more buying control, offering better prices to customers, and thus growing with customers at a faster rate. I squeezed out the competition, and that led to market confusion. We turned jobs faster and supported customers with better, more direct technical support when things did go wrong.

Not only did we have record turnaround times, better pricing from buying direct from manufacturers, easier and cleaner invoicing to our customers, better pricing due to NO KICKBACKS or commissions built in, and accepted POs via text message, but we were fun to work with. People liked us and remember, **people buy from people they like.**

Defining your Ice is knowing exactly what sets your product or service apart from all the others. It's the why when someone decides to go with you over your competition. It can be a collection of things adding up to making you the right decision or in most cases it is one particular thing that sets you apart. Know what it is and use it, abuse it, and keep giving the audience what they want.

11

Trait 3: Learn to Listen

About one year into building the company, I was asked by a mentor if I would be interested in having lunch with Del Harris. For those that don't know, Del was an NBA basketball coach for the Houston Rockets and Los Angeles Lakers. Del led the Rockets to the NBA FINALS and was the guy who drafted Kobe Bryant with the Lakers. I was ecstatic and of course accepted the invitation for lunch. I was like, *No way this is really happening*. That hour I spent listening to a man who was battle tested. I asked him several questions, and a few answers stuck in my mind forever. One of my questions was about leadership. It was a basic question, but it was about when I would know if I was a good leader.

Note that I did not ask Del for a secret to becoming a good leader, nor did I ask him if I was a good leader (I know he can't teach me those things). I asked him how I would know if I was a good leader. Del responded by saying, "If you turn around one day and people are following you, then you would know you are a good leader." Again, all your leadership books are only telling you tricks to perform as a leader; obviously it is not natural to you since you had to look for the answer in a book. All I wanted to know was how I could tell myself if I was or wasn't a good leader!

Such a basic answer, but of course. What I did not know was that three years later that moment happened for me. It was October 2012 and our company was moving out of the barn and into our new production facility four miles away. The guys showed up on moving day, lined up, looked at me, and said, "What's the plan?" That's when I knew I was the leader, and based on their body language and excitement for the move, I must have been a good leader. I guess four years had gone by in a flash. I guess we were around $3 million in revenue at the time and we were profitable. I guess I had my head down grinding for so long that it didn't sink in that we were in business for over four years and that our team had grown. We had about 12 employees at the time, and I knew I was their leader on that day in October. Only I had a vision for where I wanted the equipment placed inside the new facility, where the office space would be, and how the flow of the operation would work. I was pulling the strings and leading the team toward the future vision of the company. In fact, when I signed the lease for the new facility, I signed a first right of refusal on the property to the left and right of our suite number. I told the team on move-in day that I had done this, and some of them looked shocked.

I remember their faces, and I explained to them this was only the next phase in our future growth. The barn was roughly 8,000 sq. ft and the new facility was 24,000. To these guys the 3x growth of the facility was more than enough to make it feel like we were making progress, but for me to explain that I already requested the next 50,000 sq. ft. showed them I had a plan and a vision. Remember, don't sell people where you are or what you have done; rather, sell them where you are going.

People want to know there are more tricks coming and the show is not over! In case I forget to touch on this later in the book, yes, we eventually moved into all 75,000 sq. ft and then some by 2016.

Del's other piece of advice was that I should always hire people smarter than me. Do not be intimidated by others' intelligence, as they could never override the guy with the vision. He assured me that by surrounding myself with people smarter than me, they would make me look really good. Thus, I reflected on hiring and bringing on my partner eight months into this venture. My partner was my stagehand and he was book smart. My partner was a scholar in college and an engineer by trade. His analytical mind would ground my "all gas" mentality and would question my radical decision-making. Sometimes I would listen and sometimes I would go against his advice, but at least he was there as a second voice to hear. After my partner was hired, my next hire was my sister. If anyone was smarter than me, she'd be the one. I was reminded every day growing up that my sister was so much smarter than I was, and her ability to go through college and turn a profit off of grants and scholarships proved it.

With these two new additions to the company, I was stacked with smart people around me, but like others they looked to me for the vision. Like the others they were following me! Together we climbed out of that barn and into our initial 24,000 sq. ft. facility in 2012. I guess every magician has qualified people helping him pull off a trick. Don't fear if one of those people can overrule your vision, but have confidence they can assist you in getting there.

The ability to listen is essential to your growth as an individual, but applying what you hear and recognizing what is going on around you is key. Along with listening, have your head on a swivel. Be aware of your surroundings and look for signs of whether or not your direction is meant to be. It was early 2013, the city of McKinney wanted to do a ribbon cutting ceremony at our new facility. On that day we invited local customers to show off the new facility, city representatives like the chamber of commerce and city council, etc. We passed out Popular Ink T-shirts and celebrated the next step in building the business. Not thinking anything of it, we went on about our business. About a month later my wife and I went to church on a Sunday morning. The pastor of our church directed everyone's attention to the big screen and said they had a mini video put together of all the baptisms they had done recently. It was incredible. In a short span of time they had baptized over 300 people who had never found Jesus prior to our church reaching out past our city lines. As cool as that was, what my wife and I saw in that video gave us goosebumps.

Keep in mind early 2013 means we had moved into our newer and larger facility in October 2012. My first two months' rent was free on the new facility space, thus December was the first month I had to pay the new higher rent bill. To say the least, our old rent payment at the barn was $1,000 per month plus electricity. The new payment was nearly $10,000 plus several utility bills. There was a lot of uncertainty and doubt in my mind about whether or not we were healthy enough to take on the additional expenses.

But there we were. Watching this video in early 2013 at our church. And in the video, much to our surprise, was the pastor baptizing people, wearing my company T-shirt! What? Is this a sign? My wife looked at me with confusion. I returned the same look to her. Why was he wearing a company T-shirt while baptizing people? I took it as a sign that I was in the right place, doing the right things, and that everything was going to work out. I later emailed the pastor and asked why. His response was that all of his Hope Fellowship shirts were dirty, and he had to have a black shirt as everyone else was wearing black Hope Fellowship shirts that day. Our shirt was new, clean, black, and presentable. Thus, he baptized people in our shirt.

Learn to listen, but not just to words. Listen to the signs of the atmosphere around you. Listen to your instincts to help you make decisions that have no certainty in them. Faith is a huge factor in making sound decisions in a quick and effective manner.

When you listen, don't just absorb the words you hear. Turn those words into something. Make wine out of the water you are given! When signs show you that what you are doing is right, go hard. Go harder. Go for it all! What did I have to lose if fate was on my side? If only I was this wise year's prior maybe, I would have accomplished success sooner.

I can recall 22 months into building the company and it being a Wednesday in the middle of April. I remember calling my partner into my office and telling him we had no cash in the bank. It was 48 hours before payday and we had two employees. How were we going to pay these guys their wages they rightfully earned? Payroll would be roughly $5,500 if my partner and I wanted to pay ourselves that week as well, or we needed to at least scrap together $2,000 to pay the two employees.

As the day was coming to a close, I told my partner to not worry about it. "It will work itself out," I said.

My partner responded, "How is it going to work itself out?"

I replied, "I will think of something."

The next morning, we came into work as if nothing was wrong. We stuck to the production schedule and our daily tasks when suddenly a package arrived. It was an envelope that had been overnighted to us from a guy in Connecticut. I immediately tore it open and out of the package fell a letter, a ziplock bag, a check for $6,000, and a CD-ROM disc. I know most of you probably don't even know what a CD-ROM is, but back in the 2000s, that is how we transferred large data such as art files, music, etc. The ziplock bag had powder all over the inside of it, and it had a packet of some sort inside as well. As I opened the ziplock bag, I pulled out a partially sealed packet. I then read the letter, which in short said:

> *Dru, I am currently having my packets filled at Hormel's Wisconsin division. The most recent run of my packets have been leaking all over the country and it is destroying my brand's image. I believe you know Barb at Hormel and she said you could fix this issue for me. If you can, time is of the essence as I need film printed and delivered ASAP! I have enclosed my artwork for you to process and a check so we have no delays. If the check is too much, hold on to the balance as we will order monthly from you. If the check is not enough, I am hopeful this prepayment will not delay the order shipping as soon as it is done. Please hurry.*
>
> *—Jay Klein*

I sat back in my chair in disbelief. First of all, this was a referral. This being a referral means I had someone like Barb believing in me and having confidence in me to solve a problem that they needed solved quickly. The reason the packet was not sealing was obvious to me, but to other sticker printers they had no idea. In the industry there are several films that look alike, but all work a little different when it comes to seal-ability. I pinched some of the powder between my fingers and rubbed them back and forth like a detective would when finding a powdery substance. The powder was dusty, with bits of granulation in it, and there was a lot of powder for such a small packet. There were two things that could be done to solve the problem. The packet either needed to be increased in size to accommodate for the powder to fall naturally to the bottom of the packet before the top seal was sealed, or you needed a more aggressive sealant. The standard film that the previous printer chose had a generic sealant on it, and when you seal through granulation or a lot of dust, you need a premium sealant that will find itself no matter what. When any powder is dropped to the bottom of a pouch or bag, you have what we call "kickback," which is the dusty poof you get when dropping the powder into the packet. When that kickback gets in the way of the sealant, you lack a hermetic bond. In order to get a hermetic bond, I immediately went to the most aggressive sealant possible (Ionomer). Ionomer will seal through nearly any contamination or powder in the way. By upgrading Jay's sealant layer, I printed those packets in less than three days and shipped them to Hormel. Jay was a customer for over nine years before we outgrew him; he spent over $1 million with me over the life of our relationship, but none being more priceless than that first $6,000 order.

As I held the check, I showed my partner, and he asked me what we were going to do with it. I said, "You are going to go cash it! We just made payroll!" There are countless stories that every entrepreneur has like this and there is really no explanation. It's a miracle, to be honest. These little miracles, when handled with charisma, make you look more and more like a grand illusionist. Don't freak out, but know that somehow the sun will come up tomorrow. Listen to others when they are giving you words and apply those words to make a difference. Listen to your surroundings and your faith and at times accept the unexplainable when it happens. Checks don't just show up on your doorstep at the most critical hour in your company's history; why did it happen to me? Did it just happen, or did I have anything to do with that illusion?

12

Financing the Act

Throughout our growth we were constantly challenged with financial issues. When we were hurting for POs, we were burdened with debt. Before we even started, we were behind the eight ball with little wiggle room. Money could have solved those issues, but we had none. When we needed to improve our equipment or make an investment to expand our capabilities, money could have fixed that as well. The result of these situations gave me a hard knocks education in how to build a business with no money. I dabbled in a little bit of everything from hard asset lenders with extreme financing terms, to personal loans with personal guarantees, factoring, and so much more. I would have borrowed money from the mafia or cartel at the time had I known anyone with connections.

Our primary way to build the company was **factoring**. If you are unfamiliar with **factoring, it is a method of obtaining cash for purchase orders.** Not all industries qualify for factoring, but typically a manufacturing company or a company producing a hard asset or textile is a good candidate. Basically when a customer sends in a hard PO, you forward that PO to a factoring company. The factoring company takes the PO as a hard contract and extends you 80 percent of the PO's value in cash immediately. The 80 percent cash extension on a $10,000 PO was $8,000. With that $8,000 in cash in our account, we could then reserve raw materials that we had to prepay due to our weak financial situation. Yes, by 2011 we were profitable, but things were still tight, and please recall what the state of the economy was like from 2008 to 2014.

Even though we were profitable, imagine if you get two or three POs in at one time and each of them requires raw materials of $20,000 or more. In this case you would need $60,000 cash in order to obtain the raw materials needed to produce the POs, as well as several other expenses that are fixed or variable, on your monthly P&L. Even with two profitable years under our belt, we were too high of risk for a traditional bank to invest in with a line of credit, and we continued to factor every job.

By prepaying our vendors for ink and raw material on that $10,000 order, we would be left with about $3,000 of the initial $8,000 cash extension. That week we would make our payroll for our few guys with the leftover reserves from the factor, but then we were at $0. We would then bill for the PO in full when the job was complete, and when the customer paid the invoice, they would pay the $10,000 to a PO Box owned by our factoring company.

Our factoring company would take 2 percent of the $10,000 plus their initial $8,000 they extended us. Thus, they took $8,200 and deposited $1,800 into our bank account. The factoring company took 2 percent for 30 days of extending cash against a hard PO. It was rough, but we made it work. In the end we saw $9,800 of the original $10,000 PO. Statistically a business that leans on factoring during startup phase has a life expectancy of five years if they are lucky. We beat all odds and eventually we stopped factoring. I remember our factoring company calling asking why we weren't factoring anymore. We were able to respond by telling them we were so cash heavy that we no longer needed them. We got cash heavy by getting so many POs at once on a consistent basis. Consistency is key! We were hot as a brand, and we continued to stay hot for some time.

Remember this: **SALES CURE ALL! This is rule #00 in building any business. SALES CURE ALL!**

At other times during our growth when we couldn't fund a capital investment, we would borrow money from friends or family and pay them 20 percent interest. When you do something like this, you have to fully believe you're doing the right thing. When we bought our second press, the only lender that was willing to look at us was a hard asset lender.

A hard asset lender will make you guarantee interest even if you pay off the note early…which is what we did with this press. Hard asset lenders also take first position on other equipment you may own that would counterbalance a default on the loan. Within two years we were able to pay off the note, but still owed five years' worth of interest to the lender. Do what feels right and don't second-guess yourself. Do not *ever* second-guess yourself. So we overpaid for an asset. That asset helped me play a more elaborate shell game, attract new customers, and ultimately become a millionaire. I'm not going to play the nickel and dime game even if the nickel added up to $200,000 more in interest. I'm sorry I wasn't born into money, but I won't apologize for doing whatever I had to in order to pull this trick off.

What other choice did we have? Our financial backer (the Developer) was a poser! He was broke! We knew we had to get creative and take some unconventional methods toward navigating financial decisions. Use all the resources available to you and ask around how others accomplished getting over the funding hurdle. There are SBA loans, bank loans, personal loans, factoring, hard asset lending, etc. Use the method that best suits you.

13

♠

"Tough Lesson in Business Ethics, Kid"

So you may ask what ever happened to the Developer. Well, when I met him in 2007, he was worth roughly $20 million and by 2011 he was broke. I'm going to backtrack a little here. It was June 2011 and the Developer asked me to come visit him at one of his real estate offices for an impromptu meeting. When I arrived, he sat me down for a talk. Basically all of his investments for the past four years had gone belly up.

I attribute this to him being an idiot and never paying attention to his businesses. Remember this advice: **MIND YOUR BUSINESS.** He trusted too often and was not smart enough to see the bigger picture. As an entrepreneur, no matter how big your company gets, stay involved. If you want to be a silent investor, then be that, but as an entrepreneur, you have to grip the steering wheel and control the company! As a silent investor, you know your risks, so don't act surprised when you lose your money. As an entrepreneur, you should know everything going on in every department and every phase of your business. You need to consume yourself with all the minutae and know where every penny is spent.

I often describe the Developer as the best mentor I ever had, as he showed me everything not to do. Perhaps that's how I became successful at such a young age. While other entrepreneurs typically fail their first, second, or third time, I didn't. Perhaps that's because I simply made decisions based on the opposite of what the Developer would do. I had no respect for this man and used that instinctual compass to guide the business.

In this impromptu meeting the Developer told me he was in a tight spot and would need to reconsider our sweat equity deal as the printing company was the only asset he had that was in the black. Remember the real estate bubble from 2008? He lost everything. Thus, he and his friend would be taking over the printing company and he would no longer need me or my partner. I was confused. I was the reason the printing company was an option. I had rebuilt the company with my bare hands! I was the reason it was an option! How unethical of a human!

This guy was the devil.

He was a liar. He was the reason all of his businesses had failed. He was the reason karma was biting him hard right now. I immediately told him he had no non-compete with me and that none of the customers would stick around if I was gone. I wanted to hurt him. I was filled with rage. This was a pivotal moment where I decided to store the vengeance in the top drawer of my filing cabinet! I stored this away as future Dmotivation. I stored this away as future fuel.

I was selling myself hard, and he agreed. He realized I was right. He then said that it would be me, him, and his friend building this company, and I looked at him like he was crazy.

He wanted to dilute my hypothetical 49 percent to 24 percent and share 25 percent with his friend and keep 51 for himself.

I could have taken that deal. I could have been twenty-eight years old and accepted it by looking out for only myself, but I had a guy in the barn with me for over three years and I owed him respect. In this moment I realized as a man that I had **integrity**. I declined the Developer's offer and said, "I guess this is it, then." Besides, how long would he have used me and then just thrown me to the curb with 0 percent real stock? He had shown his true colors, and one piece of advice is once someone shows you their true colors, get rid of them.

I immediately drove back out to the barn, closed my partner's door to his office, and explained to him what the Developer had just proposed. He was in major shock, as the Developer was someone he looked up to, because he was the guy who talked him into moving to Texas, he was his ex-girlfriend's stepdad, and he was his mentor. For me it was not as much of a shock. I was always a pessimistic person and I was always waiting for people to let me down. It all seemed too good to be true despite how hard we worked to get the company off the ground.

People like me don't become millionaires, I thought to myself in that moment. This was the world's way of righting a wrong, as I was surely on my way to becoming a millionaire, but remember, you're not supposed to be able to leave your faction. What was I to learn from this? What could be the positive here? Doesn't it always seem like right when you get ahead in life, something knocks you back down? Have you ever got a tax return for $750 and a day later get in a fender bender that cost $751 to fix? It's the laws of nature at work, right?

A few days later and I had a one-on-one session with the Developer's friend, who was supposed to come take my job. I looked him square in the eye (a father of 3, a husband with a marriage that need some work, and an owner of other businesses) and I told him there was no way he could do my job.

I emphasized that the Developer was overselling him on the opportunity.

I described to him that the company was an unorganized work in progress, and I clearly explained the amount of sleepless nights I had, and that my average day started at 3:00 a.m. There was physical work needed and I was not sure he could take that on. I must have completely turned him off, as the next day the Developer requested another meeting. This was the meeting where he realized he had nothing if I was not involved, and I immediately told him I would buy the printing press from him, but I would not pay him for my book of business. He later agreed and by August 11, 2011, my partner and I owned the company outright.

Trust your instincts.

Not all magicians are good people. In the real world most people are not good. This is a sad fact. In fact, some of the most corrupt are the ones that try to cover it up in plain daylight. **Don't ever trust a businessman, entrepreneur, or magician who carries a Bible into a business meeting.**

Don't ever trust a salesman, businessman, or anyone who mentions their religion or God in an introductory meeting. In no way, shape, or form should you leave meeting someone for the first time and know what religion they are. Anyone with a fish symbol on the back of their car is more than likely compensating for something. In magic there are props to cloud your perception and focus. **The Bible in the hands of a businessman or a fish on the back of his car are distractions.** The intent is to make you get a sense of peace knowing this person is a Christian or biblical in some sense, but those who know this trick know its intention. Take it from me, the most unethical people I have ever met in business are ones who use psalms in their company mission statements and those who carry Bibles into business meetings along with their iPad.

All magicians have an element of cheating. Magic isn't real! All entrepreneurs or businessman in general deceive people, but the thin line is if your intent is malicious. Your heart is your greatest and only tool to balance out your mind. Never let greed or selfishness cloud who you are in business.

In 2009 I landed a printing project for the brand Playboy. I did not deal with Playboy the brand, but someone who had licensed the rights to use the bunny on the side of a 2 oz. energy shot and a 2 oz. libido shot. The brand took off like wildfire at local 7-11 gas stations, Big Lots, and several department stores. The owner of the company licensing the logo always carried a Bible with him. When he spoke to me, he would quote Bible verses and explain to me why and how he made all his money. He also carried a gun on his hip, as Texas allows open carrying of a firearm. After about a year of the project going strong, something happened. More than likely, the man probably did not pay the licensing fees to Playboy, and more than likely they came after him and shut him down. Unfortunately, I never did get the whole story, and worse, I was left with over $70,000 in debt, as he filed bankruptcy on that entity and walked away free and clear! In fact, he disappeared into a cloud of smoke and went on to build his next company. Doesn't that sound like something a magician would do? That's the life of an entrepreneur.

I should have known that a man with a Bible who was doing business with Playboy had no morals. The man never had to pay me the $70,000 he owed me for printing those labels. That's America! In 2009 this $70,000 debt could have closed my business, but I navigated the course the best I knew how. If I think about it, I remember the Developer and his friend Nathan always carried Bibles into their business meetings and put them on the table in front of them during every meeting. To this day Nathan owns another business now and has a verse from Psalms written on his product. Be smarter than to contribute to people's well-being who are this corrupt.

I immediately picked up the phone and called the vendors I owed money to and explained that I had been left high and dry. I explained the customer filed bankruptcy and that it severely crippled my business. I explained I would not be able to pay the debts I owed them within the terms they had given me, but I vowed I would pay them at some point. I explained I needed them to work with me. I needed them to understand and help me avoid filing bankruptcy myself. Besides, who would win if I filed bankruptcy? If I filed bankruptcy, they, too, would never see their money, but if they allowed me to slow pay when I could, at least they would get their money eventually. I had my partner call the vendors weekly and give them updates.

If I owed them $70,000, I offered them $500 for that month. I was slow paying when I could, but ten months later I paid off the $70,000 and came through on the commitment. I learned a lot about credit profiling and a lot about my instincts. I knew that guy was trouble when I met him, but I wanted the revenue. I wanted the business! Just like you, there will be times of desperation, and all deals sound like a good deal. In the beginning I will spare judgment, but when you are healthy enough, be smarter!

My advice is to be selective when you can be about who you allow your customer base to be. For sure, in the beginning I get it; take everything you can, as **you have to stay in business to be in business.** However, when you get to that healthy stage in your business, nearly all successful business owners fire certain customers and focus their attention on the ones who are either less maintenance (say no to high maintenance customers who drain too much of your time and resources), those customers with bigger profit margins, or perhaps those customers who show appreciation for what you provide. Don't be afraid to fire customers when you get your company stable.

In addition, do a thorough job when profiling your customer for their credit terms. Don't be afraid to ask for 100 percent prepayment on first-time orders, 50 percent deposit on second-time orders, and gradually make them earn net 30 terms. This isn't the wild west. This is the world in the twenty-first century with a million loop holes to duck and dodge a contractual obligation such as debt. Make your customers earn their credit, and protect your business from going out of business due to others' poor business management. Learn how to develop that sixth sense in business and how to navigate away from the corrupt magicians.

14

♠

Ethics, Act II

Since we are on this topic, let's talk about ethics and morals a little more. Please understand that there are consequences for being unethical, and as an entrepreneur/CEO, you take the fall for the Sleight of Hand when they are not pulled off correctly or if they are deemed illegal by society. If you're simply an employee and your company is found to be unethical, you are legally not liable; you get to walk away, and you may lose your job, but in some cases (Wells Fargo!) you get to keep your job and life goes on. Business is all about pushing the boundaries, but if worse comes to worse, you are the one who is liable. As the CEO, you are the one people sue, people want to see arrested, people slander, and more.

Take the CEO of Audi for example. Rupert Stadler was the CEO for Audi when he and his supporting cast devised a plan to design, install, and sell Audi vehicles with a software that would trick diesel emission testing. Basically, they temporarily pulled off a trick that reaped them huge rewards by selling several thousand vehicles that did not meet the safety and emission standards. This saved them costs and made them more profits, as they could cut corners. "Nice try, Rupert."

When a vehicle of theirs was hooked up to a piece of emissions testing equipment, the vehicle software would kick in to give it a passing grade! Genius, right? Wrong! In 2017 someone figured out the trick, and by 2018 the FBI had tracked the roots of the trick back to Rupert himself. In 2018 Rupert was arrested and put in jail for his choice to be an unethical magician!

For every one trick that gets caught, there are billions that do not. In business it is about risk and reward. What Rupert did was something he was taught to do by his mentor or by being involved with several businesses over the course of his career. At fifty-five years old, Rupert found himself behind bars and his life was forever changed. You must understand the consequences you face when being an entrepreneur as well. In 2018 Audi was fined $25 billion in retribution and damages.

In 2015 Audi had revenues of $58 billion! Thus, paying off a $25 billion fine is nothing! The show can go on and no one feels a thing at Audi. Audi profits a net profit north of $4 to $5 billion a year. Audi can easily finance their way out of this "slap on the wrist" with a low-interest ten-year loan from their financial backing. Thus, no job cutbacks, no slowing down in capital investments, etc. Audi can pay cash for this! Is that fair? Remember, the rich stay rich, and the tricks will keep coming as we make it acceptable and easy for the bad magicians to get away with things. During Rupert's time as CEO, his compensation was so much that once he gets out of jail, he is so rich he never has to work again. This is why magicians and business owners alike go for the big score. Even if you temporarily have success, it is often enough to stay ahead for life after being busted.

Bear in mind, being the bad guy does not take you making

an unethical decision to accept responsibility, but sometimes your product may accidently hurt someone or cause damage. In these cases, you are once again liable. Do the ethical thing and accept the responsibility as much as you would accept the rewards if everything was perfect in the world. As the entrepreneur, this is a part of the risk you take when being a risk taker. It's not just financial risk, time risked, but all liability risked. If you stay within the moral and ethical lines of business while pulling off a Sleight of Hand, then you have nothing to worry about. In my journey I never had anything to worry about, but for many magicians, you are the Board of Director's bulletproof vest. Even if you have investors, a board of directors, or executives under you, it is the master magician who takes the bullet and does the jail time. While you take the bullet, the Board replaces you with a new magician and the show goes on.

Do you think Audi's next magician will be a priest or a businessman? Audi's next CEO will be all the magician Rupert was and more. Companies of this size will always keep refining their act and looking for ways to fool the audience for their gain. Just what will it be that they do next? Did Audi disappear? Nope! Audi is still going strong, but with a new magician at the helm!

Doesn't the Sleight of Hand craft contradict having integrity? NO, I'm here to tell you that it doesn't! For over a decade I was faced with a lot of decisions and a lot of opportunities. Every time I made a choice I made the ethical choice.

In manufacturing things have to be done consistently, and you have to rely on all your employees to do a task the same again and again. People make mistakes. The human factor is the hardest to calculate and predict for. The one thing you cannot control in business is the human factor. Several times when we were starting out, we made mistakes. Several times there were judgment calls we had to make on quality and if we would send something out to market.

Perhaps the print was the wrong color, slightly below acceptable quality, or perhaps we had lamination issues with the film, or curing issues. Sure, we have shipped unacceptable product before, but it was on accident and something my team missed while checking quality. Remember, these machines rip at high speeds, and humans will have an error rate.

What we would do and what we would learn from these rejections or quality mishaps would improve our processes. Never in the time I was the leader did I send quality out the door that was below par intentionally. In fact, I remember a run of print we did for Kyani (a great MLM company out of Idaho) and we had a process breakdown in production. The internal rejection cost us $250,000, but it wasn't worth risking Kyani's brand image or ours. That's integrity! Over the course of 12 years we threw away over $3 million worth of bad print instead of sending it into the market. It took us this many mistakes to perfect our processes and procedures, but every time I did this my team saw my integrity and they saw what kind of integrity I wanted to be at the backbone of our company. *I say, perfect processes and procedures loosely as all processes can always be improved, but they got to the point where we at least knew what we were doing.*

I trust our guys so much, and I view the culture to have so much integrity, that still to this day I do not lock my office door. We are open 24/7, and I do not have a lock on my office door. I don't take from my guys, and I trust they will not take from me. Do you know another CEO who does not lock their door?

There is nothing in my office that would give away my

tricks. A magician does not leave a trail of bread crumbs when he vanishes. Be as transparent as you can be with your team and they will be that way to you.

It is rare to find transparency in business, and even when there is a level of transparency, please know you're not being shown everything. Remember Southwest Airlines? These deceiving business tactics are so common it is scary. Just do the right thing. Be ethical and do things that your grand-mother would approve of. Being good is a choice, but being good doesn't just mean you will find success. Remember, good things don't just happen to good people. Contrary to what people think, I have a saying, "Good things don't just happen to good people. Good people make good things happen." I have willed everything that has happened in my life. I never sit on the sidelines and just pray about it. It takes more than prayers. God gave you the ability and the freedom to make choices. It's a choice and the more power you have, and the more responsibility you are given, the greater the impact of your decision to be good or bad.

15

The Beginning of a New

From August 2011 the company was mine. The name was new and our future looked brighter. We continued on for 11 more months in that barn, but that breakup with the Developer led to our move off that farm and into that real industrial park in October of 2012. Remember the move and how I found out people were following me?

From 2012 to 2018 everything I was doing was so simple to copy, but no one else was able to. I was using today's technology and disrupting a dinosaur industry of gray hairs with it. In our facility all of the machines have an iPad. You may think that's simple or common sense, but apparently not. The iPads allow each machine to communicate with one another and allow the operators to communicate with me directly. The iCloud calendar was accessible from my iPhone, and when sitting in Utah, I could have a customer ask me for a quick turn on a job.

In front of that customer, I could pull out my iPhone and add a job to any machine. For example, if I select the 16" Comco calendar on my phone and add a job called

"7-11 Energy stick lemonade part #3354 at 1 million sticks/ PO75893," then simultaneously three iPads were notified back at the Texas plant. Instantly my job preparation department's iPad was sent a notification of the job that was just changed and put on the calendar.

The CSR (customer service representative) department's iPad also notified them of the change. Instantly, with no one talking, a CSR issued a work order to production, the job prep department pulled the customer's plates, the ink department blended the ink for the job, and hours later the job was on press running. This is called **market disruption**…and it was free. To my customer they think I'm a magician pulling off the impossible, but it's just using tools readily available with today's technology. No one else was doing this. Our fastest turn time ever was two hours. It was crazy to come through for a customer like that. What we realized years later was that people would pay so much more for this type of service, and we were able to charge a premium in times of crisis—something we called a PITA ("Pain-in-the-Ass") charge, but wow, were we thrilled to have those PITAs on our monthly P&L!

So here we were…unique from the inside out. Inside we were purchasing smarter, producing more efficiently, we were faster, we were viewed as more credible, and we were more reliable and better liked by our customers. From the outside the brand was vibrant.

Now we were popular! Our taglines on the back of our shirts read, "Because it is a popularity contest!" I meant for that tagline to take a shot at the greedy "gray hairs" who owned this industry prior to our arrival. That was a jab about who was on top now. Our culture was a disrupter for many of our competitors. I was building a company by not only putting the customers first, but also putting the staff first! If you treat people well, they will perform well and in turn your customers will get better and more consistent quality. I repeat, *If you treat people well, they will perform well and in turn your customers will get better and more consistent quality.* Happy customers mean growth!

I was giving bonuses, buying the team shirts, buying hats, painting our facility in bright clean colors, revamping the website to be cooler than industry competitors, hanging posters in the production warehouse to make it feel like a hangout spot and not a production facility, bringing in a cus-tom-made pool table with our logo on it, arcade games for the break room, vending machines, huge flat screen TVs with DirecTV for the team to catch up on shows or watch sports during their breaks, installing an indoor basketball court, corn hole set, etc. We were noticed by our industry magazine in 2016 as "The Google of Manufacturing" in America.

My vision was to bring that Silicon Valley feel to a blue-collar industry. It was disrupting. We had people applying to come work at our facility due to the culture. We had people accepting less pay to be a part of our culture. Our competitors' top talent was running to us, begging for a job. We once interviewed nine guys from a competitor ten miles away, and five of them cried in their interview. No lie! They cried because they wanted out of the dictatorship they were in at their current job. They were tired of being belittled by their boss and especially on the shop floor in front of their peers.

Don't treat people like that! You can't build a business without people, and know they will make mistakes. When they do mess up, that is your opportunity to win them over. How will you handle it? I had to mature and grow into the natural leader I am today, but I never belittled anyone or reacted in a rude manner to a team member directly. Sure, I was boiling when mistakes happened, but the damage was done. This is how you build that market-disrupting culture! Sure, I lost my cool behind closed doors and I showed my frustration at times on my face, but I never directly disrespected an individual.

All around we were different.

We were the new kids on the block six to seven years later, but we were the best and we kept getting better.

16

Free Publicity and Strategic Marketing

What gives someone credibility?

What gives one brand more recognition then another? Advertising! Your ability to "set the stage" must be spot-on. Advertising and publicity are like lighter fluid to any fire. Advertising is the stage being set and the product selling itself through demonstration or persuasion. Advertising is setting the ambience of the room. What kind of buzz is around your brand and how do you get it? How much does it cost? Ask me how much I spent on advertising a year, and I'll respond with an average of $600 per year for the first nine years of the company. The $600 were for really cool business cards that were made of plastic like a credit card, and I simply put this expense in the advertising account because it was excessive and it did help me when handing out business cards at events. People were shocked at the quality of our business cards and it helped the brand's image have that premium look. That's it. So how did we grow you ask? How did we advertise? How did we get sales with no sales reps?

TRICK #6: **How do you get others talking about you without talking about yourself?**

I have said it once before and I will say it again, "Word of mouth!" Word of mouth has, and always will be, the number one way to advertise. The reason this is true is because if someone tries a product and becomes a believer in it, they are bound to talk about it. For us, we did not turn to Facebook. No Twitter, no mass email programs, no social media at all! Not to say social media can't be used as a tool, but for us we did not choose to use it. In fact, if you put too much time and resources into social media, you forget to look up and you take your eye off the ball. I do know some people who choose to use it, but it takes discipline, and you as the entrepreneur should probably not be the one assigned to managing the social media if that is an avenue you go down.

People trust other people's feedback and will often let their guard down to go purchase that same product or service, but should they? Word-of-mouth advertising is free to you, the company, and the question becomes how to create that buzz around your brand. Think about today's world and what YELP does for a consumer. Collecting reviews of "real people" and selling that information is the ultimate vehicle for referral-based decision-making. Or is it? Did you know there is a trick for that? Most don't! There are memberships you can buy on websites such as ReviewTrigger and ReputationStacker to enhance and boost your positive reviews on Amazon, Yelp, etc. There is even a market for those that want to make extra income and write negative reviews. Think about that. The competition can pay to get you bad-mouthed. If you're a restaurant owner or a service provider, how do you survive these Sleight of Hand? Think Angie's List and the confidence you have with hiring someone for a project that is Angie approved. Should you feel comfort or confidence with the

Angie's seal of approval? That is a source of referring someone of preference over another, isn't it?

(P.s. Yelp, Amazon Prime Choice, etc. all use business sleight of hand! They are pushing those products because they get kickbacks or get paid a bonus for an influx in sales on those items.) THIS IS A SLEIGHT OF HAND! ALL OF IT! EVERY DAY WE LIVE IN THIS WORLD OF THOUSANDS OF SLEIGHT OF HAND! You can't get away from it.

Do you remember at the beginning of the book when you read through all the accolades I had received? Do you think they just happened on their own? Would you be shocked to hear most of it was free, and I caused it by asking for the publicity? You should not be shocked. Remember, Chevy pays for those awards, and I guarantee there are awards in your industry as well that you could purchase to get you some sort of accolade. I would literally write to magazines and ask if they needed a story to tell. You can do this too for your own business. Write or call your local newspaper, TV news networks, blogs, and magazines. These media outlets need content, and you would be shocked how many of them will listen to you. The more you have your story fine-tuned, your rebuttals, your answers to questions, your resume of work rehearsed, your truthful hyperboles, and your ability to ask without asking, then you will see how easy free publicity is. When I say "know your resume of work," I mean know what would make someone interested. What makes you original and what makes you convincing? Be confident.

The first magazine I was ever on the cover of was *McKinney Magazine* (30 minutes north of Dallas, Texas). I contacted *McKinney Magazine* and asked to be featured. I told them a sexy story about two guys in their twenties who had built a multimillion-dollar printing company in McKinney, Texas. (At the time, we were $2 to $3 million in revenue per year, but saying we were a multimillion-dollar company leads them to think something far bigger). Remember my advice about letting people assume what they want to assume? I explained to the magazine how it would benefit the city's desire to recruit new startup companies to the area. How confident I was when saying the word *multimillion* was the determining factor. With confidence, people inflate their belief of the word *multimillion* to mean over ten to twenty million. Had I been less confident, they would have questioned and asked specifically how many millions. In response I sold the story so well I made the cover of the October 2012 issue. I was named Success Story of 2012 in *McKinney Magazine*—a small local magazine, but it looked very professional. I had multiple issues of the magazine framed and hung in my lobby. I also mailed several hard copies to customers, competitors, and suppliers in the industry. It just so happened that the cover of October's issue also boasted *Money* magazine's logo on it, as McKinney had just been named the "#2 Best Place to Live in America!" I blasted links of the article to all over in a humble manner, thanking everyone for allowing me to achieve success. I was not coming off as arrogant or bragging like people do on Facebook. I was saying, *Thank you for helping me achieve this level in my professional career,* but at the same time I was letting them build on their illusion of what I was becoming.

The tone of my emails and the message when I answered interview questions for articles always had an underlying strategy to them. I was and I am always one move ahead of my audience. When people read about my success, about my story, and connected their opinion to who they thought I was, I never wanted to leave them with an inkling of a reason to not like me. I was humble, appreciative, and always pushed credit onto others. There was strategy to this from the beginning. I was my own publicist. Like any celebrity or public figure, they are told how to act and how to answer certain questions. As an entrepreneur, remember you're putting on an act and you will be under the microscope by many to slip up somewhere. Be aware of this, and form a strategy for how you will answer questions about success and how you will let people see you in the public media outlets that surround success.

Once you land your first magazine or publicity accolade, it becomes easier and easier to get featured in other formats. McKinney Vision was an online YouTube news channel that quickly asked for an interview, and I accepted. From there I then blasted both the magazine article link and the YouTube interview link to new and existing customers. I linked those articles to our website under the About Us tab. Every move was strategic and calculated. I hit customers who I felt were distancing themselves from the brand or that I had not heard from in a while. Remember, I did not have sales reps, so I was at a slight disadvantage with how often I could get face time with all the clients we had.

After McKinney had been tapped out, I reached out to *D Magazine* (a Dallas-based business magazine that carries a lot of clout in Dallas) and asked if they were interested in following up on the story of a North Dallas company based in McKinney, Texas. The editors at *D Magazine* assumed McKinney had done their due diligence on our company, which made it an easy decision to basically rewrite their story, but add some more substance.

The *D Magazine* article was released in April 2013, and in June it was followed up by an article from my alumni magazine at the University of Cincinnati. The UC magazine was a rag-to-riches story that helped me gain instant credibility when you googled Dru Riess. All of these outlets were the result of me stirring up the publicity. All of it was me selling my story and making it sexier and sexier each time I was interviewed.

As you read all the articles, each one has a bit more substance and each one makes you form your own opinions about how successful I was becoming and how quickly it was happening. The question no one asked was if it was true or not.

In December 2014 I was featured on the cover of our industry magazine, *Flexible Packaging Magazine*. The editor at the time and the article I sold starting in September of 2014 was how dominant we were and how market disrupting we were to the industry. This trade magazine followed our industry closely, and you have to imagine the writers were bored with the same old story lines.

Our story was so unbelievable it was refreshing for the people writing it. From 1,000 miles away, the editor writing this article was eating out the palm of my hand, and somehow I was so convincing she titled the article in the December 2014 issue "Top Printer of the Year" by *Flexible Packaging Magazine*. I could not believe it! I had sold her that we were the best, and now it was in ironclad black-and-white print all over the internet in our industry and in magazines all over the world. We were named "Top Printer of the Year" by our industry magazine!

The phone began to ring and we got calls from Kellogg's for real this time. Many more calls came, and business was easier than ever, as there was no selling needed at this point. After the *Flexible Packaging Magazine* in December of 2014, we rode the wave of momentum until my instincts told me I needed more publicity. It was August of 2016 and I picked up the phone to call *Flexible Packaging Magazine* again. I knew the editor had moved on from the 2014 article and that someone new was in charge.

I knew this would work and it did. I told the new editor about the previous article, and he went back and read it. I asked him if he would be interested in following up on that article and if he would like to be the first to feature the company again because so much had changed in 16 months. I told him we had more than explosive growth (which was true) and that our angle this time should be about the unique culture our company had and it should pose the question, Why don't other companies treat their people the way we did?

I pushed that we had spent over $3.7 million in capital investments for new equipment and facility expansions, and that we were looking to start buying other print companies across the country (maybe true). I explained how unique the culture was with the arcade games, pool tables, basketball court, sky diving events, rock climbing walls, bounce houses, etc. I explained to the editor that I was thirty-two and I had a fresh new look on this blue-collar industry that my "gray hair" competitors could not fathom. Being thirty-two, I grew up watching the era of Silicon Valley be built and I basically implemented the illusion that we were "Repackaging Blue Collar." Why couldn't blue-collar manufacturing in America also have enjoyable work environments? No seriously, why can't it? Why does blue collar get the stigma of a lunch pail, hard hat, uncomfortable work conditions, and grease on your hands? The editor was in love with the article, and just 18 months after being named "Top Printer of the Year," we were featured on the cover of *Flexible Packaging Magazine* for the second time! This time the article was our company nickname: "The Google of Packaging."

After the second article in *Flexible Packaging Magazine,* I went for the jugular. I picked up the phone and called CNBC. Four months later I was featured on CNBC on a primetime TV show called *Blue Collar Millionaires.* From the airing of the show, Dallas Morning News came calling and did an article on us in February 2016; and *Dallas Business Journal* named me a top "Power Player" in all of DFW in their December 2016 edition. I shared the cover of the December issue with Jerry Jones on the cover! Imagine that. In 2007 I moved to the greater DFW area without a car, $500 cash, and a 500 credit score, and in December of 2016 I am being named a "Power Player" in all of the DFW area. I was a rising star, a businessman, and an entrepreneur/magician to keep your eye on.

All of this publicity, all of this buzz, all of it was me moving the balls under the cup one at a time. Each time I was featured in something, I made sure to use it to get it in front of potential or current customers. The illusion of who Dru Riess was and how successful I was grew, but no one really knew the truth of what I was worth and how big the company was. Early on I registered our company on Manta.com and other business websites, but then never went back and edited the information. The information I put on those websites was inflated to where I would build the company in the future; and I eventually did! I put what I wanted people to see about our company on those websites and made sure it always leaned toward the company growing. I led the audience once again and made sure they knew bigger and better things were still to come. I kept the details to myself, but I allowed the articles, interviews, videos, and websites to cloud people's judgement and form their own opinions. When defined in business terms this is what a Chief Marketing Officer is paid to do. This is business!

You can do this as well. Why wouldn't you ask for the publicity? Why wouldn't you advertise your story?

With all the free advertising came more accolades. In 2016 *Inc.* magazine named our company to the *Inc.* 5000 list as one of the fastest growing companies in America. In 2016 the SMU Dallas 100 named us to the top 100 companies in the DFW area. In 2017 both the Inc. 5000 and SMU Dallas 100 named us to both lists once again.

In 2017 Ernst and Young named me (Dru Riess) a final-ist for Entrepreneur of the Year in which I lost due to local politics, but still, to be nominated and named a finalist for Entrepreneur of the Year for all of the USA is nuts. In 2016 we were a Gold Trophy winner at the American Business Awards and 2017 we won a Silver, both for "Manufacturer of the Year," beating out companies such as Toyota. However, every time one of these things happened, the brand image grew, the confidence in the customers grew, the confidence in our staff grew, and I knew exactly what I was doing.

In late 2017 more magazines called, more articles were written, Fox News called, NBC called again, Rob Lowe's TV show called, Kathy Ireland's TV show called, and many oth-ers continued to want to feature the story and find out more about this company that rose out of the ashes. By 2018 the marketing and advertising was on autopilot.

In late 2017, when I needed to accelerate the amount of new business coming into the facility, I finally spent some money on a marketing campaign, but it was extremely specific. I stra-tegically and specifically targeted decision-makers at large corporations. My campaign involved three Apple watches and one Xbox. I handwrote four letters to four individuals. The Apple watches got a letter that said, "Let's stop wasting time and start solving your packaging issues." The Xbox got a handwritten letter that said, "Let's stop playing games and start doing business." The letters went on to quickly give the highlight reel of our company, and our capabilities, define our ICE, and list accolades we had received over the years, then closed with a personal signature from the Founder/CEO of our company (ME)! That campaign cost me almost $2,000 and amounted in more than $5 million worth of yearly revenue and then some. That is called strategic marketing! Imagine going into war and knowing you have four enemies and only four bullets. Use them wisely and don't miss! Be creative! Be original! This was creative!

For the rest of my industry, they spent $20,000 to have a booth at each trade show in Vegas, Chicago, and Anaheim. For my industry competition, they were working harder and trying to force-feed their brand to the market when we allowed the market to tell our story for us. Do you think those four new individuals that received a free Iwatch or Xbox will share who we are, and can you imagine how much word-of-mouth business will come from landing those four new powerhouse companies as customers? Get an ROI if you're going to spend the money advertising.

17

Mind-Set and Self-Talk

As I have said fifteen times by now, where you came from financially and socially doesn't have to be the reason you don't succeed. No matter where you are in life or what you've been through, you can take those moments of defeat and success and use them to fuel your vision.

You can use words of advice, pressure situations, and more to navigate life when the waters are rough. Turn those moments into a thick rope that you can rely on. I have used every put-down, every letdown, every minute spent on the bench, every snide laugh, every smirk, and every fake conversation to fuel me. Don't get discouraged by those things, but rather encouraged.

Laugh and move on and continue to build your dream. Cry and move on, but continue to build your dream. Your success will be determined by your mind-set and self-talk. Remember "Framing" and how you speak to a customer? Framing goes for how you present something to yourself as well. It's all about what you say to yourself in the mirror when no one is looking. At what point will you realize that there are no strings holding you back? And if there were, I guess people like me cut them the same day the doctor cut my umbilical cord.

Do you remember the movie *The Matrix* when Neo was at the Oracle's house? The little boy was staring at a silver spoon and bent it with his mind. Neo then asked how he did it. The boy said that he did not bend the spoon as there was no spoon to bend.

"Wait! What? No spoon? You mean no silver spoons either?"

At what point will you step into the center of the stage and realize that you are the magician and the props in this world are yours to manipulate? Here I am, having never read a real book, and now I'm writing one. Here I am, a kid who was street smart, and now I'm book smart. I may not know physics or trigonometry, but I'm smart enough to put my ideas on paper, and you're reading them.

Your mind-set determines your trajectory. I had to eventually realize that those kids in my hometown were not better than me and actually did not have a spoon. I had to realize that I was more determined because I was challenged more than they were growing up. I was prepared to overcome more than they would ever be able to. I was carved from a stone that they would not stand a chance against in the real world outside those Southern Ohio borders. This is mind-set!

I had to realize that if it ever came down to me vs them that I would not shy away from the opportunity to outwit them, demolish them, pulverize them, or simply outhustle them. This is a mind-set! How did I get there? I'm not sure, but I did. By the time you get to the end of this book, you should feel like you could reach right up your sleeve and a bouquet of flowers could pop out. At the end of this book, you should see the correlation between magic, business, and the world of boundaries that do not exist if you do not let them. Being a leader, being a business success, and being a market disrupter is all about mind-set!

How ironic is it that now that I've achieved wealth, my own kids will be labeled as those hypothetical silver spoon children? I guarantee, with intentionality and presence of mind, that I am going to make sure they are grateful for every meal they have, that they are kind to others, and that they have purpose and know what it takes to succeed. I will coach my children to have a mind-set that is hungry for their own success and full of desire.

If you're rich and you ask your dad for money to start a business, you're not an entrepreneur. You never will be! An entrepreneur by my definition is someone who takes risks! Period! What is the alternative for a rich kid who fails? Oh yeah, still rich. If your dad leaves you a company and now you're in charge, you're not an entrepreneur. You're a job sustainer. PERIOD.

Maybe there are exceptions to this rule, but this is my mind-set. This is how I think in my early to midthirties. This book is for trailblazers, rainmakers, divergent individuals, and the underestimated. This book is also for people who are not trailblazers, rainmakers, divergent individuals, etc. This is not for girls whose dads golf with George W. Bush weekly and start popcorn companies for fun. This is not for those whose daddy made some calls and got you on *Good Morning America*, *Oprah*, and several other media outlets. Sorry, but you're not an entrepreneur. You're simply a rich girl born into the starting blocks of lane 1 and using all the resources your ancestors provided for you. Good for you, but don't you dare claim you're an entrepreneur. Real entrepreneurs would eat you for breakfast and if given a level playing field would leave you a peasant. Listen closely: my daddy never made a phone call for me to get where I am. There are a ton of talented people in this world who never get an opportunity because of the politics game, but I pray I am an example to those who want it bad enough. You can achieve what you want even if the odds are stacked against you.

Again, we can't blame our parents, but we sure can make sure our own legacy is one that elevates our own children and grandchildren to be born with strings in their hands. Stop dwelling on the past. No matter who you are, you can rise up and make it if you play your cards right. The past is the past, so don't allow history to repeat itself for your kids and their legacy. Can you become the master magician?

How do you talk about yourself today? Do you vocalize your limitations of being the ball under the cup? Do you portray to the outside world why you are not where you want to be? This is negative self-talk. Is it repeating what you heard people say about you as a child or during some of your lowest moments in life? Stop doing it!

People respond to confidence, smiles, laughter, leadership. Can you feel my passion in the words I have chosen for you? Time is the one thing you cannot buy, and it is constantly winding down. Don't waste the time you are given. It's all about mind-set and the way you live. Show people the best you! Give us all something worth being around and make us want to pay for your time! You are special, but only you know how special and what you are capable of. Society wants people to fail; people enjoy people who are beneath them. People less fortunate make others feel good about themselves, so don't let them have any fuel. Show no weaknesses and have a superior mind-set.

18

Do You Want to Own a Job or a Business?

Remember there are magicians who do kids' birthday parties and there are magicians who sell out auditoriums in Vegas. In other words, do you own a job or do you own a business? I can't count the number of times my wife and I meet a new couple and we ask what they do. The wife replies that her husband is an entrepreneur. I immediately think, *Oh really?* Come to find out, he brokers insurance from his home office, or he and another guy write software code in a 1,000 sq. ft. office space. In my opinion yes, these guys are entrepreneurs.

They eat what they kill and have no safety net for a down month. How about a plumber? All sole proprietors or craftsman? Yes, I suppose; however, I view this type of entrepreneurship as the magician who plays at kids' birthday parties. I view this as owning a job and not a business. Once you stop working, in those scenarios, your business dies.

Another way to look at this is to ask yourself what kind of pilot you are. Leading a business and navigating a business can be done more than one way. You can be conservative in your decision-making, rational, emotional, calm, aggressive, and more. When you run a business, is it predictable? You can often rely on a commercial airline pilot to get you from Sacramento to Los Angeles. The commercial airline pilot or CEO of a corporate company will stay between the lines, seek multiple people for approval on decision-making, get supportive data to stand by his/her decision-making, and more than likely is a predictable person. When you run a small mom-and-pop company, you can be loose with your flight log and departure times, and often relate to a local airport with private planes coming in and out daily. Small companies built to stay small can get by with fewer processes and procedures. Less red tape.

In my case I'm Maverick from the movie *Top Gun*. I'm a fighter pilot who makes quick decisions, and once a decision is made, I don't look back. Explosive startup companies, market-disrupting companies, and revolutionary companies require a business owner like this. I often buzz the tower, and I accept people disagreeing with my decisions, but stand by the decision I make. I don't have time for data, and often a matter of seconds could mean life or death. Entrepreneurship and leading a growing business takes instincts, and I trust those more than any other tool to be my compass. I rip through each day at a fast pace, and I run a company that will win more than we lose. I do things the right way, and I intend to always get it right, but sometimes the jet crashes and burns. Fortunately, fighter jets have an ejection seat, and I often get myself out of the predicament that my style gets me into. On a commercial flight there is no ejection seat, no trap door, and thus with all that supporting data and time lost gathering approvals, you better be damn sure you do not make the wrong decision. As a commercial pilot or a corporate stiff, it takes longer to recover or change directions when the wrong decision has been made.

So what kind of magician or leader do you want to be? How big do you want it to get? To be a master magician you have to remember owning a job is not the same as owning a business. Owning a job means the business, the show, the journey is over when the entrepreneur stops performing. Owning a business is David Copperfield or Houdini; it is any entrepreneur that scales a company and builds a brand larger than themselves and exists beyond the founding magician. I know guys who run a company with 30 plus employees and still own a job.

There is a certain level of talent it takes to scale a business or know what to delegate and when to delegate it for your organization to mature. The bottom line is, "You don't know what you don't know." Remember, entrepreneurship does not come with a playbook. Are you looking for the Vegas Strip or the flexibility of simply being your own boss? Both of these avenues come with their own level of stress and pressure. Both avenues also come with their perks. Small-party magicians deal with less HR, people issues, and training of new staff, and they only eat when they perform their tasks well enough for payment.

The big-time magician manages layer upon layer of the business and has a lot more legal responsibility, more mouths to feed, a board of directors to report to, shareholders to appease, entertains a larger audience, and more difficulty finding the inefficiencies or weaknesses in the business, etc.

Scaling a business is an act that is not suited for everyone, as people naturally plateau. **The same people you build a $5-million business with are not the same people you will build a $10-million, $20-million, or $50-million business with.** This is fact!

Know the difference between being the stagehand and the magician. **A stagehand owns a job no matter how high up**

the totem pole he or she is at an organization. There is not more than one magician in any company. It takes a really special person to be an entrepreneur and to build a sustainable, scalable, and solid business.

If you have been around a good entrepreneur, really ask yourself, Was I even needed to pull this off? What was my role? Was I a prop? Were you instrumental in the business's growth or merely an instrument to fulfill an act in the show? I was once asked by my business partner if I thought I could have built this company without him. I replied, "Of course not." It's the truth, but I did not share the other part to the answer. I could have done it with a million other people.

I needed a stagehand. Everyone does. People are needed to build a company, and you cannot do it alone. Don't be so arrogant to think that you can accomplish greatness by yourself. You can't. Have you ever heard the saying that it takes a village to raise a child? Same for a company. Once again people have plateaus, and you have to be capable of noticing when they have reached their pinnacle. If you don't want to just be a job owner, your instincts and ability to make quick decisions will increase your chances of scaling a viable business.

It is your responsibility to lead and to make tough decisions. It is your responsibility to have that vision and intuition about the rhythm of your business. In 2017 I split ways with my business partner of nine years. I brought him in eight months after I started building the company and parted ways when I felt a lack of rhythm in the performance. It was a tough thing to do, but for me to reach my full potential and for the act to get any bigger, it was an action that had to be done. Thus I had to find a stagehand who was capable of bringing the act to the next level!

As the master magician and entrepreneur, you either commit yourself fully to achieving greatness or you own a job.

When an obstacle is in your way, you deal with it. You cannot go around it. You must grow from every experience and get better and better at making decisions. My business partner is a friend and a brother despite how he may feel. Though he may have a hard time understanding his place in this world right now, he was appreciated during his tenor at the company.

Nothing worth doing is easy, but your commitment and ability to execute is where you set yourself apart from the job owners. Some magicians are so good they make those around them feel as if they are the illusionist, as if they are the rare talent, etc. It was hard for my partner to understand the company could go on without him, but eventually it became a reality to him that it could.

TRICK #7 Have you ever gotten someone to do something or come up with an idea that was your idea? Have you ever got someone to agree to do something you wanted them to do by making them think it was their idea? This skill takes finesse and a good entrepreneur is a master at this.

Five years into building the company, my ability to create ideas in other people's minds allowed me to plant the seed in my partner's mind that his way to bring equal value was to watch over the company at night. The goal was to not lose money on night shift, and he did just that. It is essential you know your role. Accept your role and don't lie to yourself about what you are to the organization. If you're the magician, you know where the trick is going. If you're the stagehand or job owner, you're just waiting for your next assignment.

If you're fortunate enough to be around great magicians and prosper with them, then ride their coattails, but know your role and show appreciation for them letting you come along for the ride. Also, don't overstay your welcome and be respectful when it's time to get off at the next stop. Only master entrepreneurs can scale a company and get it beyond owning just a job! Do you want to own a job or a own a business?

19

♠

Act Like You've Been Here Before

In 2015, at thirty, I was light years ahead of most of my peers when it came to responsibility, finances, dealing with pressure, and having a grasp on who I wanted to become. From an early age, I saw myself being famous, a person of importance, a special person held to a higher standard than my peers.

Maybe it was my imagination, but it was also my internal expectation. Anything less and my life would have been a failure in my eyes. In fact, an internal vision for yourself can be called your mind-set. This was mine. Though I immediately envisioned this, it did not come from a pompous place. Because I envisioned this, I was humble about it as it was nothing new to me. At thirty I had several million dollars put into my possession from selling some shares of my business to a private equity firm. *A **private equity (PE)** firm is an investment manager that makes investments in privately owned companies through a variety of loosely affiliated investment strategies, including leveraged buyout, venture capital, and growth capital.*

On day one I put the money in a hypothetical "vault" and ignored it. I still ignore it. Unlike young professional athletes who act out of character because they are given a lump sum of money for the first time in their life, I stayed grounded. I don't talk about it. I don't tell people about it. I have no Facebook or any social media presence at all! No Twitter. No Snapchat. Nothing. Never have I had a Facebook or any social media presence other than a Myspace account that I deleted in 2006 prior to starting my company. Thus, when this life-changing day occurred, I went home and my wife and I cooked dinner together!

Remember, I wanted to turn off any external ricochets from reaching me and put myself in the best position to succeed long term. No distractions.

What I do is for me. What I buy is for me or my loved ones. What I do is for my family. No one else needs to know about it. When I meet new people at my kids' school, my neighborhood, or close-knit community and they ask what I do, I don't even tell them I am or have been a CEO, founder, or president. I simply say I'm in the XYZ industry, "I manufacture packaging goods" or "I help people gut-check themselves for success." That's my answer. Vague. Sound familiar to other strategies of mine? Again, everything I do is calculated and, though hard to believe by some, purposeful. Why do they need to know more than that? Believe me, you will be okay if you don't tell everyone about how successful you are!

On the opposite end of the spectrum, I watch other entrepreneurs not know how to handle the success. From strip clubs, to bottle service at night clubs, to social media sites, to sketchy dating sites, and posting images of themselves on Facebook bragging about experience after experience they get to do. I watch these people look for love in all the wrong places and with all the wrong strategies. If your pickup line is telling people you are rich, then you will attract the wrong type of people. I have seen it with men and women. It's almost like you're so insecure that the only way you think people will think you're worth their time is if you can pay for it. "Act like you have been here before!" These people will have selfish intentions and the relationship will be one sided.

I watch other people who have come into money put $30k into new cars by upgrading the stereo systems and doing anything to draw more attention to themselves. I ask, **"What the hell are you doing? It's a new car! It has a new radio already in it!"** I have watched a guy come into money, and within 24 hours he hires a personal concierge to book reservations at restaurants, buy taxidermy as decorations for his home, hire personal shoppers, and more. Literally overnight I have seen people go to this default setting that was somewhere within their DNA that makes it clear they cannot handle success. These "new money" individuals act out of their original character, but have reality distortion to it while it is happening.

Prior to having money, did you use to buy your own clothes? Prior to having money, did you use to make your own reservations by picking up the phone and asking for one? *Hell, opentable.com is a thing now. You don't even have to call!* Did you collect dead animals before? Did you wear pocket squares and three-piece suits to Applebee's before? Who can't shop for their own clothes? Who can't call and make a reservation at a restaurant? Please refer to the age-old saying that we all put our pants on one leg at a time. As a successful person, many doors will open for you, and yes, you will get opportunities that ordinary people will not get. From flying private, to VIP access at sports games, meetings with celebrities, and more. However, in each of these experiences, **act like you have been here before.**

Don't come off as the rookie in the room. It may not appear

you are doing that, but you are! Don't come off as desperate or excited. Sound familiar? So many of the things I mention about being confident, blending in, not being desperate, and always putting on an "act" should become second nature to you as more success comes your way. Don't ask for autographs! Don't ask for pictures with a celebrity in passing! Aspire to be asked for your autograph. Don't ask to take a selfie, but rather aspire for others to someday want them with you. I watch how people handle themselves in these situations and it's pathetic. I watch how "new money success" or spoiled people who inherit their resources talk and treat people like they were beneath them. Don't be that person. Don't be the person who is one way to certain people and another way to others. Don't have an SCF.

The **Sunday Church Face** is a coined term to reference those who pretend to be Bible Thumpers, but behind the curtain are at a strip club in Vegas the night before. In other words, don't be two-faced. These people are hypocrites, and that is what "new money" individuals who can't remember where they come from are.

In 2017 I was having a dinner at Del Frisco's Grille in Plano, Texas. I knew the manager, as my family and I are regulars at the establishment. It was a busy night during the week and the upstairs loft was closed off. I told the manager (Andrew) it was a little loud for me to accomplish what I needed to accomplish at this particular dinner, and he asked if I would like to go up to the loft. I replied, "Sure, that would work." Walking up to the loft, I could see someone else was upstairs. Once I got upstairs, I noticed that it was Vanilla Ice.

He was having dinner with family and friends. I immediately went into "Act like you've been here" mode. Sure, there was a small part of me that was like, *No way, how random, no one will believe me.* But then I realized, for all I know he is looking at me like, *Who the hell is this guy? He must be someone!* I realized that it didn't freakin' matter who would believe me. It wasn't something I needed people to know. It was my experience, my moment. As I approached my table, I thought, *They don't just let anyone up here on the weekdays.* I liked that.

I often refer to myself as Bruce Wayne. I like the idea of having two identities and people not knowing the other me. I'm not two-faced, but there is a side of me I let all the public see and then an additional side to me that is an enhanced version with more detail. To know I have the success I have, to know I have financial security is my secret identity and only something my close loved ones need to understand. To everyone else in this world, I want to appear as the man among the people. I'm not as fancy as Bruce, but the aspect about Bruce I want people to relate to me as is the kindness he has when in his street clothes, how approachable I am, and how humble I am.

Who you are as a hero is simply an amplified version of who you are on a daily basis! Who you are without money should be an amplified version of who you are when you come into money. Know your purpose and know the kind of individual you want to be to the outside world. If you do have a $25,000 shoe collection, no one cares…keep it to yourself. Seriously, no one cares! Besides, you can only wear one pair of shoes at a time. If you watch my episode of *Blue Collar Millionaires* and compare it to all the other episodes, you will see a distinct difference. I went back and forth with the producers about how they would frame me and it was from a family guy, dad side, non-materialistic guy. Yes, they made me throw out a few dollar values for a playset I bought my kids or the house we lived in, but I intentionally kept close to the vest.

All the other entrepreneurs that they featured bragged about all the things they have, and you will see in my episode I do not. I knew exactly what I was doing and what I intended on using that exposure for years later!

Keep what should be secret in your book of secrets. Not everything about you is something people need to know. Be humble! Approach each day with humility and a level head about your life being just as delicate as the person next to you. Look yourself in the mirror and ask if you are this person. Or are you the idiot that thinks all 3,000 friends on Facebook care about you? **Act like you've been here before!**

Lastly, on this topic of "Act like you've been here" I want to give you some pointers for things perhaps you don't know or encounters you may come across in which maybe you have not been there before. No joke. I wish someone would have told me these things, as these were awkward but real moments of coming into success.

1. An artichoke is a rich person's vegetable that they like to eat with lunch or dinner. The only time I had ever heard about artichokes were when I ordered spinach and artichoke dip at TGI Fridays or some sports bar. I had no idea what the natural state of an artichoke looked like or what other meals were made with it. There is no substance to it as I was at a dinner one night and there was an odd petal of some sort sitting in front of me. Everyone put a few on their plate as the dish was passed around, so I did as well. I then placed an artichoke petal in my mouth and started chewing. I chewed for what felt like forever. The texture was tough and hard to bite through so I muscled it down and swallowed quickly. I then looked around, and other people were placing the artichoke in their mouth, scraping it with their teeth, and then placing the petal back on their plate! I immediately realized it was like edamame and you were not supposed to eat the

outside of the artichoke petal. You were to scrape with pressure the substance inside the petal into your mouth and then place the shell back on your plate. How embarrassing, but I had never been there before. This was a first for me. I hope this saves you if you encounter the same thing. An artichoke is not something you cook to be filling; it's simply a delicacy, and regular everyday families are not going to put this on their dinner plate, as it adds cost and gives very little return.

My wife also had this exact same experience when she went out to eat with the high society woman of our neighborhood for the first time. They ordered artichoke as an app, and she had no idea what to do with it. When she came home and told me, I couldn't stop laughing. I was relieved I was not the only one, so I pass this wisdom on to you. You're welcome! I just saved you a potential embarrassing moment.

2. Wine tasting is a serious matter. The piece of advice is to always be the last in a group to try the wine. Leave the glass on the table and wait to see what others do in the group. Pick the glass up and stare at it, then take and put the glass down on the table and gently swirl the wine. Act as if you're looking at the color and tell anyone that asks that you're "opening it up a little bit" by swirling it around. I have no idea what that means, but I still do it. Apparently, it needs to breathe! Ha. I love wine. I drink a lot of it, and I enjoy the rarer and more expensive names as there truly is a difference in the experience, but for the most part, I just drink it because I like it. In a group of people, you never know who knows more than you, so just take it slow. Watch the others and see if they tilt the glass and point it up toward the light looking for the richness in color or the "fingers" of the wine dripping back down the inner part of the glass. I have been to Napa and Sonoma several times, and by now yes, I know the proper steps to swirl,

sniff, and taste. I know what I am tasting for now, but in the beginning, you may not. Hopefully, this advice helps you "act like you've been here before."

3. Tip well! Don't be a douche bag. Respect the service industry and "act like you've been here before." I was a server at several restaurants in college. I treat people how I wish others always treated me when it comes to tipping. I once served Andre Agassi, and he was so cool and appreciative. I also waited on TJ Houshmandzadeh (NFL wide receiver), and he stiffed me on a $200 check. Twenty-five percent or more is good! Even if the server sucks, tip them 20 percent. This is how they feed themselves, and though they may suck at the job, don't leave them empty-handed. They will figure out they suck soon enough, but that next utility bill or that next meal has to come from somewhere.

20

Fun Facts

My fun facts are facts about life that should be obvious, but that no one seems to be aware of. Remember, street smarts are more valuable in entrepreneurship, as nothing is planned and a lot of it is impromptu. What may be common sense to some is physics to others.

Fun Fact #1

Magicians are magicians, and entrepreneurs are entrepreneurs. Nothing less. Understand that when you meet an entrepreneur, you are meeting an entrepreneur. You are not meeting the person they really are. As an entrepreneur, I am in costume at all times. I go home and 90 percent of my façade is put down, but there is an element of stress and an element of my disguise that stays on. It simply can't come off. I often tell my wife that she will love me someday. She smiles and says, "I already love you."

I respond with, "No…you will actually love *me* someday." Unfortunately, my wife met me eight months into this show (eight months into building my company) and though she knows me better than anyone in the world, she has never seen Dru without the pressure of building this company on his shoulders. She has never seen me at zero stress level or a normal person's level of stress. *A normal person's 100 percent stress is equal to 1 percent of an entrepreneur's stress. For an entrepreneur, everything is amplified and the stakes are always higher.* She has never seen just how goofy I can be and how likable I truly am. All entrepreneurs are like this. Imagine if financially the company is in a slump, do you run home to your wife and make her worry with you? Yes, your wife is supposed to be your rock, but you don't share things like this with her.

That is a perfect example of her not getting 100 percent Dru. On a night like that she might get 70 percent Dru, as I will be distracted, stressed, worried, in deep thought, analyzing, and trying to figure a way out of my work situation. This is the life of an entrepreneur. I told you it's a commitment to be a master magician. You can never let your guard down and you cannot trust anyone. There are horrible people in business. There are people who act like they like you and will use you. There are people who will share anything you tell them not to. You will get people shopping you out for a better deal even though you feel like they are your best friend.

Be secretive and don't show your cards to anyone; you can never be fully transparent and show how your tricks are done. Keep an element of mystery and keep your audience on their toes. Have an element of mystery that entices your customer to stay engaged and committed, as they don't know what you will do next. Stay reserved if someone asks for proprietary information even if they say it's not to share with someone else, but for their own knowledge. I call BS! I knew when someone asked me the breakdown of a film structure, that they wanted to shop me out to my competitor. I made it damn near impossible to do so. I would lead them down a dead end by sending them fake acronyms and fake data sheets for our material. No forged data sheets, but data sheets that were coded in a way only my team could decipher.

When my competitors tried to quote it, they would price themselves out of the business. I essentially made the competition quote oranges when I was providing apples! *Sleight of Hand!*

Fun Fact #2

PTSD is real. Remember earlier in the book how I described the everyday life of an entrepreneur? *Becoming an entrepreneur, and the everyday life of an entrepreneur, feels like you're the magician standing on the stage preparing for his grand finale. The day-to-day life feels like being handcuffed and lowered into a glass casket filled with water. Every single day feels like this! The key is thrown to the bottom of the casket and the lid is sealed shut with padlocks and heavy chains, then covered with a large cloth as the audience waits. This feeling never goes away until the day you retire, sell the business, step down, or die.* Sure, on some days you suppress the feeling and enjoy the moment. Yes, you will have great days along the journey that make you numb to the stress as the oxytocin, serotonin, and dopamine in your body temporarily mask the stress. When I closed a million-dollar deal, nothing on that day could upset me, but the next day is the next day. Joy fades away and the stress and the reality of you being stuck in that casket resurface.

These pressures and stress levels compound on your body and mind. The result of carrying this responsibility changes you—your temperament, your demeanor, your focus, your memory, and your ability to disconnect change. At night you will stay up worrying, thinking, innovating, and trying to revolutionize your company. At night you will awake from a peaceful sleep, at times shaking, crying, sweating, etc. It is no different than a soldier going to war and being acclimated to a situation such as eating quickly, shoveling food in your mouth because you don't know when the next bomb will go off; and in turn, when you come home, there is a transition period to readapt to normal living conditions.

Anyone—aka entrepreneurs, not just soldiers of war—who are put under extreme pressure for a lengthy period of time can develop PTSD. Entrepreneurship does this. How you cope with it will save your life. Every time you stress, worry, or get worked up, cortisol is released into your body. Cortisol is very bad for you and is the cause of many cancers. Aside from the dramatic analogy of cancer, your blood pressure can rise and cause stroke, heart attacks, and more. Your health is something you have to put as a priority as an entrepreneur, but how do you make the time? This is something I still struggle with to this day. I was willing to sacrifice my life for success, and when in the trenches that was the manner in which I attacked every day of building the company. I was okay with death if it meant dying while trying my hardest.

Nowadays I have to ask myself, What is the point of building greatness or building a legacy if you die before you can enjoy it? I guess I would answer, *I didn't do this for me, but rather those that will follow me such as my daughter, my son, my future grandkids.*

Are you sure you want this?

Does it sound as good as ABC and NBC make it sound? Is it still sexy to be your own boss, or wouldn't it be nice to let others worry about this stuff and just collect money for a task, then punch out for the day? I have told you that as an entrepreneur it never ends.

There is no punch-out. You will find yourself eating dinner

with your spouse and not hearing a word they say. In my prime, I did this over 355 days of the year. It was not intentional, but the war was all I could think about. How many guys did I lay off today, how would I rebuild sales, how can I fix the fact that my right-hand guy in production left to go work for the competitor and has all my trade secrets?

PTSD is real for entrepreneurs. Look at Kate Spade and Anthony Bourdain, who both tragically took their lives after achieving massive success. These two individuals had wealth and accolades and friends and loved ones and business success beyond their wildest dreams, but the pressure to sustain it, or perhaps the external expectations, lead to mental breakdowns. Maybe it was something entirely different that led to their individual suicides, such as an inability to cope with personal relationships, but the entrepreneur's journey is not one without pressure and it illustrates the struggle.

Many entrepreneurs struggle during down times.

I have struggled with depression when business is stagnate. The suicide is not a result of Kate Spade's husband cheating on her; rather, that was the last straw. The business and the building of her brand puts so much on you that your personal life compounds your already elevated stress level. In most cases a breakup is hard, but it is not processed as just a breakup when you're under severe pressure in other areas of your life. Seek help when you feel yourself losing control and when the business has you pushed to your limit. As a fellow entrepreneur, I'm asking you to please be aware of that. Communicate with your spouse and your loved ones. If you do not build your circle of trust with people who appreciate what you are sacrificing to be an entrepreneur, you risk ending up like one of these catastrophes.

I had dinner with my old business partner six months after he moved on from the company, and he told me that he was just starting to sleep through the night. He told me how he was just learning how to control the ticks, the chewing of the side of his face when in deep thought, and the anxiety that was no longer there. He was learning how to be normal and remember he was just the stagehand. Never was his anxiety as high as the entrepreneur's. Imagine the decompression process I will have to go through this someday when I put my jersey in the rafters. I'm aware of how hard it will be, and I look around at the plethora of business owners or high-stress individuals who do not make it to retirement due to the PTSD. Whether it's an illness, stroke, heart attack, or suicide, these are all results of the high stakes life of an entrepreneur.

Think of the wherewithal that I have to warn you of this. It's real. My war is almost over, so how will I handle it? Only time will tell.

If death does not take me, then I am sure to battle PTSD as I learn to coexist in society as a regular guy someday. Be aware of this and trust the process. Surround yourself with supportive people who understand why you are the way you are and will have patience for your rehabilitation.

Fun Fact #3

In your lifetime you will only have at the most five true friends. I mean, five real individuals who would drop anything at any given moment of time to come to your aid. I mean, "from the moment you meet someone until the day you die" friends. You could meet them when you are five, or you could meet them when you are thirty. From the moment you meet them, it is a reciprocal relationship of give-and-take until the day you die.

If it is not a relationship like that, then all they are is a "filler." Fillers are people who are in your life for a particular period of time due to particular circumstances. You should be able to identify fillers and utilize them more efficiently after reading this book. For example, my daughter is on a soccer team, and there are other dads who like to talk to me, grab a beer with me, and migrate to me in group settings, but they are just fillers. Even if we go on vacations with those other families for a couple years, that relationship is bound to end.

Our kids grow up, grow apart, and find other friends; thus, our reason to mingle in social settings is done. I would not call these individuals to help me if I was in the hospital or if my loved ones had fallen ill. I'm not saying I don't like them, but the chemistry for them to be a lifelong friend was not in the DNA God gave us. The majority of people in your life will be fillers. These people serve a purpose, and yes, you can call them a friend for a long time, but understand the fact that you will only ever have five (at the most) true life friends, and your siblings don't count. The sooner you grasp this, the more aware you will be of the relationships you are in and what you can get out of them.

As an entrepreneur, you will need people to confide in, people to listen to you, and people to cry on. You have to be selective in your process of qualifying your five people, and it's okay if you don't find the fifth until later in life. Be very careful and be aware of which individuals you choose in your circle of five. Choose wrong and you may find your dirty laundry aired out for all to see.

I could not possibly write this book without thanking my constants. I would not be where I am without listening to others and having the will to grow as an individual. You will need voices, and it would benefit you to have mentors and influencers from all walks of life: younger, older, different careers, etc.

You will need a better half. You will need someone to pick you up when you're defeated, as the mind is often weak until you reach your full potential.

The mind looks for the easy way out, and your mentors and circle of five push you to go the course less traveled. My wife was that and is that for me. So much of marriage is similar to building a business. You must work together as a unit, have a common vision for what family will look like, and execute each day to make progress.

My wife and I are both type A, but she is the perfect person to bounce my irrational thoughts off of. She does not judge me as she knows my heart and knows my intentions. She is strong and supportive, but at times puts me in my place. I often joke to the workforce that my wife has actually always been the CEO of the business, and I was her puppet. So many great ideas come from a woman's perspective, and so many of my ideas were sharpened and made much better by bouncing them off her first. My wife has no business experience and is actually a registered nurse, but perhaps that disconnect from business allowed her to give feedback from a different perspective on certain issues. I am forever in debt to her for walking this journey with me and allowing me to choose entrepreneurship as a career path.

On that note, the wife of an entrepreneur is not a joyous one to live. Yes, there are perks, but they are earned by being there during the gloomy times as well as the good. In addition to the gloomy times and the perks, it takes a special person to stay with a guy who continues to tell her she does not truly know me yet. It takes a special person, and you will need to find one for you to reach your full potential.

Choose wrong and not only will your marriage fail, but your business will suffer. In business, you will want to give up, and in entrepreneurship, you will look for the easy way out.

There is no divorce in business if you don't let it happen.

My wife and I did something on the altar on the day of our wedding that I apply to my business habits. On the day of our wedding, we stood before 45 people and we opened a Webster's dictionary. We took an X-ACTO knife and cut the word *divorce* out of the dictionary. We agreed to let this symbolize that it was not an option for us. Quitting was not an option. The word does not exist in our vocabulary!

We then cut that page of the dictionary out and framed it on the day of our wedding. When you walk into our home, it is the first thing you see. In entrepreneurship quitting is not an option. Period. You are the captain, and you will either sink or swim with this ship! You don't just move on to another job, but rather see it through for the good or the bad.

In addition to my wife, I had my sister as my right-hand person at the company. My sister, at age twenty-four, moved to Texas to help me chase this vision. My sister trusted me and invested in me. She went all in. I gave her $35,000 a year and looked her in the eyes and told her it would work out. Without her, the company would be missing a major part of its heartbeat. From multitasking every job imaginable she was a constant, year in and year out. During good and bad times, she stayed calm and was supportive.

She was the one I could rely on in the heat of the day, the one to accept more on her plate when everyone else was incapable. Her attention to detail and her ability to mature into the professional she is today were vital to my success. My sister would not spread gossip or show fear if she knew confidential information I shared with her. For me to have someone like that across the hall from my office was a blessing, but remember she's a sibling, so she does not count toward my circle of five.

Find people who you can gain from and be willing to listen,

even if all they ever do is combat your ideas. I had a Vistage group, a Bible study group, and a group of guys at the gym I would talk to once in a while, but I had two guys who went out of their way to invest in me. One of the first suppliers I ever met in this industry was Tim Bauer. I could not buy anything from Tim in the beginning, but he offered his time to answer questions, do R&D on different projects for me, and teach me how a seasoned salesperson talks in this industry. Tim was eight years away from retirement when I met him and had been in the industry for decades. His industry knowledge he passed on to me via face-to-face trips to Wisconsin, phone, email, and text was like getting a packaging degree from Clemson.

Tim was on his way out of the industry and saw no harm in helping me become more knowledgeable. It would be four to five years into knowing each other before we hit a business deal that was mutually beneficial to us both. His time invested in me ended up amounting to nearly $40 million worth of raw materials that I would purchase from his company from 2012 to 2017. When Tim retired in 2015, he could have been done with me, but the calls never stopped.

The Christmas cards and Easter cards never stopped. The gifts for my kids' birthdays never stopped, and I realized I truly had made a friend. I needed Tim so much to help me sound credible and to have a resource with industry knowledge, industry contacts, and more when being questioned by a customer. He was my guy in the white lab coat behind the curtain feeding me answers. I love this man and his family, and I am so appreciative of him. This type of mentor is priceless, as he was the "Industry Mentor." I consider Tim a friend, and though we do not keep in touch often, I know if I need anything on a personal level, I can call him for help.

There will be times you are asked questions on a sales call, and it's okay not to have all the answers. In these situations, say this: "Wow, that's a great question! I think I know the answer, but I want to confirm before I give you bad information. Lucky for me, I have a guy back at the facility with a white lab coat that we pay to have all the answers. I'm just the really good-looking guy they send out in the field to ask customers on a date." Boom. This answer is universal and works every time. Tim was my guy in the white lab coat. No, he was not on my payroll or back at my facility, but he was my guy I would turn to.

Next, I had my mentor, Kirk Kirkpatrick. Kirk was my second customer. He was unsure of who I was or what I was worth the first time he met me. I remember the nervous energy I had in that first sales call and how he sized me up so quick. I recall his stern but gentle threat about the quality needing to be perfect on anything I send into his facility. I remember him smoking a cigarette in his office and me walking away from that meeting assuming that was the way business was done in Texas.

From being my customer Kirk turned into a genuine friend. Kirk and his wife were 2 of 45 who attended my wedding, and he was a technical mind who had some industry knowledge in heat sealable films, but he was also a seasoned entrepreneur, salesman, and a jack of many trades. Kirk was liked by all and blazed a path with no enemies. I have no idea how you do this, so don't ask me!

I recall over the years we would meet at his favorite restaurant or what he would call his favorite—Wendy's. I recall the small Frosty, junior burger, and small chili he would order every time we met for a conversation. Kirk and I were generations apart, but it was a "peanut butter and jelly" relationship. I enjoyed hearing about his golf game, and he enjoyed hearing my stories about early day entrepreneurship. I could unload anything on Kirk. I could talk about my marriage, my kids, my mom and dad, my wife's parents, and my business.

He listened every time. He listened to the bad and listened to the good. Sometimes he would give advice and other times he would just listen. I would always want advice, but he would not always give it, as he knew me well. He would sometimes leave me by saying, "Well, let me know what happens," as he knows I was going to do it my way regardless. Kirk taught me to not react immediately when I feel an emotion. *You will have to master this trick to advance in life.* In my midtwenties I needed this advice because everything to me was a crisis. When someone pissed me off, I wanted to react, but he taught me to process it. When we lost an account or an employee messed up, he taught me to conceal the anger and process it. Conceal the disappointment and process it. Let it stir, remove myself from the situation, and think about it before reacting.

Kirk's guidance prior to me being married, after getting married, and as he saw me become a father continues to influence who I am growing into. These are the mentors and moments you cannot become successful without. This is the humility you cannot become successful without. Kirk shared his time, he shared his wisdom, and he was selfless in the way I am trying to teach you to be. No one mattered more than you when you were with Kirk. He was the one that taught me to "kill people with kindness." This mantra was hard for me, but I later mastered it and realized how it paid off in several situations.

He was a simple man with simple taste. He was a Christian, and he often led me back to the Bible to find my own answers. I recall walking his facility the first time, and during the tour, I noticed how he knew everyone by his first name. He passed on the idea to always be involved on the shop floor. He emphasized how it took 20 minutes of his day to grab his morning coffee and do a walk around the facility. He would go up to each individual and say good morning at the least, but engage in several side conversations, asking about kids, family, hobbies, etc. I stole this from Kirk. I learned this from Kirk in 2007–2008 and I still do it to this day. Whether you're my janitor, web developer, public relations manager, etc. I treat you with respect and treat you as a person. Kirk taught me this. You get more out of people when you engage.

Our facility is larger than his was and we run more shifts, but as many as I can do I do. First thing in the morning, I start my day by doing a walkthrough. I engage with the staff and am personable with them. I show pictures of my kids and I ask to see pictures of theirs. At shift change around 2:00 p.m. I do the same thing. On occasion I try to make it in during the night to pat our night shift on the back and stay involved, but that is difficult to do. It's amazing how they view you as the leader when you consciously treat them like equals.

Kirk's character will be one I attempt to mimic as I continue my professional career. On my office wall his name is etched in cursive as a sign of appreciation, along with the names of 60 other people I appreciate for assisting me on my journey. Whether they are fillers or in my circle of five, I acknowledge what I gained and how I morphed into the person I am today. All the credit in the world that I receive for building this company, for defying the odds, for becoming successful, I owe a piece to each individual in my circle of trust and even a few fillers that made my wall of appreciation. On October 22, 2017, it was no longer an option to call Kirk. There was no one at the end of the line anymore. I will forever have a hole in my heart, but I will have a wealth of knowledge to pass on in memory of my good friend.

Finally, I have my boys. I have a couple guys who have known me since I was five, fifteen, and one I met in my thirties. These are my guys. These are guys who don't judge when

I say something inappropriate and guys who can't necessarily connect to my situation, but keep me grounded to where I come from. These guys give me advice, listen, and give me a completely different perspective on situations that I may have clouded my mind from being able to see. Maybe I have all five slots filled right now, or maybe I only have four. Your circle of five will change as you grow, but I hope you gain something from understanding this fun fact and perhaps you can organize the individuals who are currently in your life. Are they fillers, or a member of the lifetime five? What can you get out of each relationship, and how will you use the time spent with each? Relationships need to be reciprocal, so invest in people, but like with all things, invest wisely!

21

Five Mistakes You Will Make

First, you will get tunnel vision.

When you have tunnel vision, you lose sight of the 360 experience at your company. Are your employees happy, do your customers get everything they need, are your competitors innovating and doing things that could be easy to instill in your brand's DNA? I know I say to not worry or focus on your competition, but keep your head on a swivel for things that are happening in the world. Don't be blind! In some cases, you may see something innovative happening in a completely unrelated industry that could be implemented into your own. In some cases, when you're visiting a customer, you could see something on their shop floor from a competitor of yours that could be implemented into your own product offering. Have an awareness about you that allows you to be in the trenches, but come up for air at times to see the world around you.

You must be open to feedback even if it comes in the form of criticism. Do not do what I do and take it personally. The feedback can be used as a compass and direct you to where flaws/opportunities may be available for improvement. Learn what a SWOT analysis is and how it is done well, and at times challenge yourself and your leadership team. When you get critics, view them as a member of the audience who was simply not impressed with that particular trick. It may not be you they are not impressed with, but rather a process breakdown during a transaction.

A SWOT analysis is a study of your strengths, weaknesses, opportunities, and threats—and is a structured planning method that evaluates those four elements of a project or business venture. A SWOT analysis can be carried out for a product, place, industry, or person. What are you good at? What is your company good at? What are you bad at? What is your company bad at? What opportunity is there for improvement? What opportunity is there for the future? What could stand in your way of being better, getting better, or reaching success?

It may have been one order that was under par, one experience that fell short of expectations, one person within your organization who tainted what could have been the perfect transaction, etc. Do not take feedback as somebody saying you are not a good magician/entrepreneur. Rather, take an inward look and find a way to modify your performance or your product.

Along with having tunnel vision and not seeing what your customers see, make sure you pay attention to what your staff sees. Make sure you have a GRIP on your culture and don't lose touch with what is going on inside your four walls. Remember that your culture is as important as the product or service you provide to your customers.

At one point I was so focused on building the business and taking care of customers, I regret to say, I took my eye off of the culture of the company. I knew better, but life happens and seasons in your business get you distracted. In twelve years I never had anyone quit, and in two weeks I had three guys quit.

I had to take a look in the mirror and ask if it was something I did. Was this trend going to continue? How do I recalibrate the culture? At home I spoke with my wife about some of my actions on the shop floor over that past month. I was stressed and I was wearing the stress on my sleeve. My team at work could see it on my face and feel it in my demeanor. One mistake after another on the shop floor was becoming too much for me to stay calm and collected, and I was putting off a vibe that was toxic. My wife suggested taking better care of myself. My wife suggested loosening up and letting the mistakes happen when they happen. As a competitor, I want to win and I want to win big. I want to win every day, but when you are building a company you are going to have losses that provide opportunities for your team to grow and learn. As the leader, I needed to let these mistakes happen and trust the leaders I put in place would use those mistakes as teaching opportunities to nip that mistake from ever happening again. I began to work out again, and about a week passed before I said anything to anyone on my leadership team about me being at fault for the culture sliding. When I did say something, I simply pulled my leadership team in the room and told them sorry. I apologized to a small group of people directly but did not address the entire company, as I did not know what my message would be yet or if it was needed company-wide.

The following week I went to the store with my daughter and bought a high-end pillow, hoping it would help me get better sleep at night and take some of the physical pain from the stress out of my body. I bought a pillow that changed my life. The pillow instantly helped me wake up on the right side of the bed! I went in to work that first morning after sleeping on that pillow with this new approach of not being as stressed out, and my body felt good. I walked around at work the following morning with positivity and greeted everyone in the facility with enthusiasm. Okay, maybe it wasn't all the pillow, but a concerted effort to dial in on a positive mind-set. My wife was so jealous she asked me to go get one of the pillows for her, and I did. Remember, my wife is an RN, and she is often on her feet 12 hours a day. She confirmed the pillow was magic! My wife was waking up refreshed and sleeping better than ever, and I felt like the old Dru again. The mind is a powerful thing!

Although my attitude was recalibrated, I could feel tension and skepticism from some of the guys on the floor. I then realized I had a bigger problem than I thought. I stayed constant that week at work, continued working out every day, and continued to get great rest every night. That Friday I learned of two more guys looking for new jobs, and as I went into the weekend, I knew Monday morning I needed to deliver a "State of the Union Address" to everyone in the company. I mulled over what I would say and how I would get through to the team. How do I come off as genuine and convince these people I was back to my old ways that had built this great company?

Over the weekend I thought, *Why would anyone ever want to leave this company?* The company was designed to be a place where all levels respected each other and where the environment was interactive and fun. We had lost that loving feeling! I then reflected on something a Navy Seal once said on YouTube. His message was about the little things in life. His message was about the details in life and how they matter. At work I was only stressed when the guys made silly mistakes, but the silly mistakes were avoidable if only they cared about the details. If I could get the guys to understand that's where my frustration was coming from, thus my negative demeanor then maybe they could accept some of the responsibility. When digging into the mistakes at work, there were processes put in place to help avoid the mistakes, but guys were pencil whipping their paperwork and not owning their craftsman-ship of the product. In short I pulled up that YouTube speech on my laptop that Saturday night. I watched the minute and six-second video of the Navy Seal who talked about making your bed.

As a Navy Seal, the first thing you learn is to make your bed. When you make your bed, your pillow must be centered under the headboard and your sheet corners need to be crisp. The idea of making your bed first thing in the morning starts your day off with you already fulfilling a task successfully. By fulfilling your first task of the day, you are setting the tone for successfully fulfilling multiple tasks each day. When you make your bed and you pay attention to the details like the crispness of your sheets and the position of your pillow you gain pride in your work. In taking ownership of making your bed, even if you have the worst day ever, you will come home to a made bed, a bed that you made, and a made bed gives you encouragement that tomorrow will be better! I loved this message and knew I had to share it. This message was about asking them to change their mind-set and not just go through the motions.

The next day I went to two different Bed Bath & Beyond locations, and I bought 50 of the pillows I had bought for myself and my wife. I brought all 50 pillows to work and put them in the conference room. On Monday morning at 6:00 a.m. I greeted my first shift and shut down the plant for ten minutes. I called every person in the building to meet in the conference room. My message was simple. I began by taking ownership for the slip in culture. Even if you're not to blame, you will need to jump on grenades at times as the leader of your organization. I talked about being a better leader and being more composed. I expressed to the team how I took my eye off the details of my day-to-day actions. At the same time, I expressed where my frustration came from, and if we as a culture could become obsessed with the details, we could build the best company in the world. I told the team what I had been doing to make myself better, as actions speak louder than words. I told them I had been working out regularly, I had changed my diet to eat cleaner, and I had invested in massages and a new pillow! I then showed them the YouTube clip of the Navy Seal giving his speech about making your bed and why the little things in life matter. I tied the Navy Seals speech in with my discussion about details and assured the team I would not take my eye off the ball again when it came to our growing culture. I asked for everyone in that room to commit to be their best self and to show respect to everyone regardless of whether or not they liked each other. I then handed them all a very expensive pillow and told them to use it as a reminder to make their bed in the morning. I asked them to use the pillow as the first step to taking better care of themselves, and the gift was a gesture from me (the CEO) showing I was all in!

I then repeated the same performance at shift change around 2:00 p.m. and again that evening at 10:00 p.m., as we are a 24/7 operation. I had one-on-one face time with everyone for the first time in over 18 months. The speech and the gifts were so effective I had two guys retract their search for a new job and the culture began to gel once again. The following weeks, months, and year were the best in company history.

So who taught me this? Who gave me the pillow idea? Who gave me the gift to collectively get people to buy into my vision and want to be a part of it? This was instinctual. I have said it before and I will say it again: "You can't teach leadership!" An entrepreneur has instincts and creatively comes up with ways to engage people for a common purpose. You can copy me or come up with your own ways to overcome cultural speed bumps, as all companies have them. This was not our first, but when they come up, you have to hit them head-on and dissolve them quickly.

Your culture is so important, yet can be a distraction at times. When you're so focused on the bottom line and the long-term vision, it is easy to take your eye off the mundane things like the cohesiveness of your organization. It's a balancing act and the hardest part of building a business. Managing people is an unpredictable chain of events. Tread lightly and keep your ear open to what is going on within the DNA of your business.

After a few of these speed bumps, you will learn to put some things in place, such as a suggestion box, an employee portal for complaints, and more. Personally, I set up an anonymous portal for our employees to engage directly with me. If they simply wanted to vent or if they wanted to tell me something going on in the shop, but did not want to throw someone under the bus, they could write a message in this portal and it came directly to my email. No one else in our entire company received these, and it allowed me as we grew to be more informed than most CEOs at 50,000 ft. in the air. It is important as a CEO that you fly the company from a macro level, but you have to hear your people and know what is going on at the ground floor. Find your outlet and don't allow yourself to get stuck on the top floor of your business with the executives who get paid to tell you what they think you want to hear!

If you recall, at one point our industry magazine put us on the cover of their magazine for our exceptional culture and our market-disrupting ways. Remember, they titled the article "The Google of Manufacturing"! You can't teach how to get your company to beat as one heartbeat. Acknowledge people's birthdays with a $50 gift card, offer a free gym membership as a perk of being employed at your business, acknowledge anniversaries of employment, have Christmas parties, and celebrate the company's birthday! All of these things are only a few things we did, but are easily repeatable in your place of business. What is culture worth to you?

Second, realize that social media can be your friend and your enemy. In my business, social media served zero purpose. Zero! None. Never did I waste five seconds on thinking about whether to sign up for a company Twitter, Facebook, Snapchat, or Instagram account. None of these in my line of work are needed. In my particular case, we sold to other businesses. We were a niche manufacturer, and our customer base was not one that would give me an ROI had I put forth resources on social media. Do an assessment of your business and make sure that efforts on social media truly give you an ROI for the resources you put toward it.

In today's business world it almost seems like an obligation to have a company Facebook account, but it is not if you don't need it to retain or attract new business. Everything you invest your time and resources into as an entrepreneur should in some way help you grow as an organization, attract new business, retain existing business, and stay competitive for years to come. This goes for capital investments and people you invest in. Everything you invest in should help you grow!

Social media is a powerful tool, but at times can cause you to have your head down when you should have your head up. Be coachable in this regard and be disciplined when it comes to doing things because others are doing it and doing things because you get value out of it. This goes for any marketing or advertising outlets. Do not just advertise to a blind audience. You would not perform for an empty room would you?

Third, hiring is a science. It is impossible to vet out people during the hiring process. You can use several resources, interviewing tactics, and more, but people will let you down. At times my intuition would tell me someone would work out perfectly in our culture, but often those same people became a virus and needed to be let go.

Be patient! Hiring is a revolving-door process in which you hope to get lucky and find rare pieces that fit a perfect puzzle. To aid you in the hiring process, understand firsthand that people are selling you their best self during an interview. Realize that how they interview is their best, and at no point during their tenure with your company will they miraculously get better. If a candidate interviews well, then so be it, but use other tools to help you figure out if they are just a good salesperson or if they are who they say they are under the resume façade.

Our company used a company called Culture Index, but there are several companies like them. I believe Culture Index to be the best psych/personality assessment. These assessments show you who somebody is wired to be from the ages eight to twelve years old.

Your natural personality traits give way to how someone's motivational threads can be pulled or triggered in certain situations, how someone may like to be managed in situations, how much pressure or workload one can handle, and more. The more you use these tools, the more you begin to fine-tune your interviewing process and polish up on the type of questions that would benefit your vetting process of an individual. Cross-linking the resume, their verbal interview, and this personality assessment truly helps figure out if the individual is cut out for the task at hand. This in depth interviewing helps you get an idea if the position fits their personality and builds your confidence that they could achieve the role you have in mind, all while meeting your expectations. Again, hiring is a process and you will swing and miss. Do your best and learn from each hire as this is probably the most common area all businesses mess up.

Fourth, no matter how well you hire for each position, it is impossible to assume everyone will get along. Hiring people is like adopting a child into a family. Each member brought into the family has quarks and things about them that will ultimately rub others the wrong way. You will most likely underestimate how hard it is to manage people. In fact, I have been asked several times throughout the years what was hardest about building my company. My answer is always the same. People! I mentioned this briefly earlier in the book, but it's true. Managing the people! I can lead and get people to do things, but no one can make people like one another. Trying to please everyone is impossible! Even with our laid-back atmosphere, a good culture, benefits, bonuses, etc. you will have backlash. I have often compared owning a business to owning an adult daycare. It is hard work and it can be very distracting when dealing with the people side of things. As soon as you can, you must remove yourself from this layer of the company. Hand the HR and people issues off to the next level of management and do not let those things distract you as the master magician. Keep involved and keep yourself informed of what the issues are and how each issue is handled, but you have to keep the distractions to a minimum when dealing with people. It would be the biggest mistake you make to get tied up and bogged down by your people-management issues.

Fifth, you will lose your cool! Listen to me: it does not do anyone any good! I mention a few times in the book to keep calm and keep your composure. I mention that the captain of a sinking ship must stay steady. I mention that a magician cannot show when he is uncertain how he will pull off a trick. On May 22, 2011, yes, I lost my composure. I had a guy run a one-color job wrong. The easiest job of the year, and he was not paying attention to the details. The result was not me losing my cool in front of that employee or in front of the production crew, but rather in my office alone. After I saw the mistake, I quickly totaled up the mistake in my mind to cost me over $20,000. That $20,000 in 2011 was a huge number! That loss could have been the defining factor of us going out of business or building it to the next level.

I was furious. I took deep breaths, stormed off to my office, closed my office door, then turned around, and for the first time in my life I threw a punch! My fist gripped tight, my adrenaline at a max, and I swung my fist at my office wall as hard as I could. I was trying to knock out a title weight boxer, but instead my fist met the drywall of my office. The drywall could not withstand the force, and my fist went through the drywall only to meet a stud in the wall. My bone immediately snapped, and as I retracted my fist from my wall, my bone in my hand was hanging there on the bottom side of my hand. With adrenaline pumping, I looked at my partner and told him what had just happened in production and the result of me losing my cool. My passion had gotten the best of me this time.

My partner asked if he could bring me to the hospital, and I replied, "I'll do it myself." I didn't want to be around anyone. I wanted to be alone to vent off steam. My adrenaline was masking the pain for a short period of time as I stormed out of the facility and into my car. I headed toward the hospital, and as I was driving, I tried to put my bone back in my hand. For a second I thought it was possibly only dislocated, but that was extreme wishful thinking. It was obvious the break was a clean break in a location where there were no joints to dislocate. The pain when I put pressure on it shot through my body and was enough to make me pass out behind the wheel. I passed out while driving and wrecked my car into a car in front of me while they came to stop at a light.

When I came to, I was lying on the side of the road with

police around me filling out accident reports and my bone still dislodged in my hand. I called my business partner, and he came and picked me up off the side of the road. My partner brought me to the hospital, and when my fiancé (my wife now) showed up, she was furious! We were seven days away from our wedding date, and now I would have surgery and a cast on my hand, and surely our honeymoon would be ruined as we had to cancel all water-related activities. My partner saw my fiancée's face and said, "I'm out of here!"

I tell you this story because who won in this story when I lost my composure? No one! Who was hurt? I was personally, but also the company. The leader of the company had to miss a few days to have surgery, and what good is a quarterback if they are not on the field with their team for every play? In my case, it was a few days, but in some cases, people make decisions that leave them far less fortunate. So I tell you from experience, "Keep your composure!" If you do lose your composure, and you probably will, learn from it!

Lastly, always remember the words of Mike Tyson: "Everyone has a plan until they get punched in the mouth." I hear from employee-level people, "My boss overlooked me for a promotion" or "My company is shutting down, and I don't want to move," etc. In this case, the employee is blindsided with something they did not expect. In essence they are punched in the mouth and all plans go out the window. What do they do next? They should have a plan, but they don't. The same is true for the entrepreneur.

Many things will get in your way on a daily basis that will not allow you to fulfill your priorities. When daily things pile up and you see no light at the end of the tunnel, you must realize you are only human and only one thing can get done at a time. Prioritize what is hot and chip away at it. Chip, chip, chip away! You cannot fire everyone at once, even though at times you will want to. You need people, and firing or replacing talent is a process. Keep steadfast in the process and push on, but in the worst-case scenario that your company or vision is shutting down, have a plan. Not having a plan leaves not only your employees blind but yourself as well. The moment you get hit in the face, nothing else matters. In that single moment, you must stop as the entrepreneur and devise a plan. This is the same no matter the magnitude of the punch. In no way is it possible to anticipate every situation or have a plan for any and all situations, but when something does happen, that must be your sole priority. Once you have a plan, call your closest allies in a room and perform an act with confidence that you know exactly how to react to the recent events in your business.

Once you have a team of people moving in a direction, it becomes a lot easier to adapt and overcome anything. I learned this firsthand when our largest customer of nine years pulled the plug with no warning. Instantly 40 percent of our business was gone, and yet we survived and are still here today! We are not only still here, but we are a stronger and more valuable organization without that customer. "Everyone has a plan until they get punched in the mouth!" Remember that! Don't ever forget that! After being hit, plans go out the window and you must be able to audible!

22

♠

Selling Tricks

If you're an entrepreneur and you don't think of yourself as a salesperson, you're probably not a very good entrepreneur. I have hinted at this in previous chapters, but it's true. In fact, if you're considering being an entrepreneur, but you hate sales, you should forget about it. Selling is vital to building a business.

Entrepreneurs who start from the beginning with nothing have nothing to sell but smoke and mirrors. When you sell, you've got to know your audience and speak to the level of your audience. Have you ever heard someone tell you, "Dress for the job you want and not the job you have"? I agree in some contexts, but not all. Dress for the job you want and dress for the client you want as well. Be relatable and authentic, not weird, stuffy, stiff, or cocky. Dress the part and instill confidence that you can get the job done for your prospect.

In packaging I was selling to blue-collar people who over the years were promoted into supply chain. If I showed up with a collared shirt and a tie, I was overdressed. Do you see how that can turn someone off? The only time a blue-collar person wants to be around a guy in a tie is when he is suing someone, defending a traffic ticket in court, or getting divorced. Don't dress above your audience.

In Colorado it is normal to go to business meetings in blue jeans and a tucked-in buttoned shirt. You must appeal to your audience and come off as someone they can relate to.

Be relatable. Be likeable even if you're being fake. Even if that means being in costume!

Being relatable is what makes people like you. In the real world, you will learn quickly if people don't like you, they will just do business with their friends or the guy giving them the biggest kickback.

You better be liked! People put their guard down when they think they are among equals. Know what kind of magician you want to be and more importantly what kind of magician your audience wants.

How do you break the ice when you are on a face-to-face sales call? If you're asked how you are, you answer every time with an enthusiastic UNBELIEVABLE! It's not a lie. You can be unbelievably good or unbelievably bad, but you answer with that consistently. People assume it is unbelievably good when you say the word with enthusiasm, but oftentimes I am having my worst days when I answer that question. People don't want to see you having a bad day!

If you don't like that, answer with, "Living the Dream!" I don't know why people chuckle at that answer, but they do. I smile because not all dreams are good. People forget there are nightmares in business, life, sleep, etc. When I answer, "Living the Dream," it's often on a bad day, but I say it with enthusiasm so my positive energy lifts the audience where I need them to be in order to feel good about giving me a YES.

Are you writing any of this down? You should! Mental note: reply with an enthusiastic "Living the Dream!" or

"Unbelievable!" when someone asks how you are doing. Step the tone of your voice up a level or two when replying with these answers. I assure you it will break the ice and open your potential customer up.

Always reach for something in your surroundings such as a family picture on the wall, a fish on the wall, signed sports memorabilia, or something. For example, if your head is on a swivel when walking into a sales call and you see a bass hanging on the wall, you better come up with some stupid story about fishing and a memory you have about fishing. If you see the client is a Cowboys fan, you better forget about your family's three generations of love for the Eagles. For that next hour, you're the biggest Cowboys fan they have ever met!

In my case, I would bash how bad of a fisherman I am and how much I look up to those who know what they are doing with a hook and a pole. Was that true? No! I hate fishing. I think it's stupid and that you are talentless if you waste your free time with a string in the water. The last time I went fishing, I was ten years old, and I caught a 5 lb. catfish. I was so proud of catching that fish. If my memory serves me correct, that is the only fish I ever caught in my life.

I wanted to keep that 5 lb. catfish forever. I brought it back to my great-grandma's house and put it in a 5 gal. bucket of water. I named that fish, and I was so proud of my new fish. I then left to go to the mall with my cousins, and when I returned, I ran to that bucket to see the fish. It was gone! I asked my grandma where it went and she said, "It's out back." I asked where. She said my uncle had it. I ran out back to him and asked him, "Where is my fish?" He raised the hood of the grill and there it was. I was forever scarred and terrified, and perhaps that's why I don't fish to this day.

My new pet was dead, and it messed me up. Do you see what I just did there? I have nothing in common with this sales prospect because I think fishing is stupid, and it is definitely not a sport, but I related with him. I was relatable, probably comical to him, and I now had his guard down. I walked out of the meeting with a deal in hand!

Another great icebreaker is my token coffee story. When sitting down in a meeting, you will often get asked, "Can I get you anything?" I'll ask for a cup of coffee. **Not because I want a cup of coffee but because I want them to ask me if I want cream or sugar in it. In this instance, I'm setting up the next trick and the prospect is playing as my prop.** This is how polished I am. This is how well I know my performance. It is effortless at this point, as I know how to dictate every interaction I may encounter during the show. When they ask me if I want cream or sugar, I go into a story. Here it goes:

Customer: Can I get you a cup of coffee, water, anything?

Me: Coffee, please.

Customer: Cream or sugar?

Me: Oh no, absolutely not. Black, please. Let me tell you a quick story why. I grew up in Dayton, Ohio. Every year they have an amazing air show they put on as it's the birthplace of aviation, you know? Well, my uncle was an F16 fighter pilot for years and was chosen as the guy to fly in the Dayton airshow one particular year. He was stationed in Boise, Idaho, but got to fly his plane to the Dayton airshow and stayed with my family that weekend while he was in town. On his last morning there he asked if I wanted to come do his preflight with him. I never knew how much went into being a pilot. How much math, how much preparation before taking course, and how smart my uncle was. I saw my uncle drinking a cup of black liquid. I asked, "What is that?" He said, "Coffee." I said, "That doesn't look like Grandma's coffee." He paused, looked me square in the eyes, and responded, "That's because Grandma is a woman. Women put milk and sugar in their coffee. I'm a man!" And from that moment on, I forced myself to like black coffee. I hated it when I was a teenager, but I refused to change it. By college I had become accustomed to enjoying a nice cup of black coffee, and as the years went on, I became a coffee guru. Isn't that hilarious how something so silly being said to a thirteen-year-old can stick with them their whole life?

I always get a smile out of that story. It gets us into a comfortable conversation rather than diving into a cold conversation about what I am there to sell them on. That story makes me relatable, as I would follow up with, "How do you drink your coffee?" No matter what they say, they are now engaged and talking. I would then follow up with, "I look up to that uncle still to this day. He's ultra successful and is a pilot for Jet Blue now. Do you have any family that is military or air force in particular?" Again, it shows my patriotism, and odds are, they can relate or they will wish they could. They will see me as a good well-rounded guy with deep roots in a family, etc. This is the art of selling.

Once you are relatable and have built rapport, make sure you have an agenda and stick to it. Be concise, swift with hitting each bullet point on your agenda, and never leave that meeting without closing the deal and getting a yes! If you don't get a yes, don't you dare leave without a reason to follow up. **It's all about the subsequent visit.** You have to have a reason to come back or get back in touch. For me, if I got a maybe, I would push getting a sample roll of printed film done for them to show them my quality. This would require them engaging and sending me their artwork. This would require them awaiting my return with a printed sample of their product. Thus, my subsequent visit! Who turns down a low-risk, no risk-free trial roll? It's a win-win. If I show quality is the same and they don't have to invest anything, it gives me a reason to follow up. Or perhaps I would have a quote I have to get back to the customer upon leaving. Anything works, but always have a reason to follow up with the customer after your initial meeting!

I can't say it enough; get people to like you, be relatable, have an arsenal of stories up your sleeve ready to be pulled out at any given second. A magician does the same thing when he butters you up with some simple card tricks before the grand illusions. A magician wants you to like his candor and his presentation, and he is reading the body language of his audience to see if he has won you over before he goes for the big tricks. This is exactly what you should be doing on a sales call.

Let customers sell themselves. Immerse the customer with a depiction of who you really are and what you're all about. They buy your story they buy your product. Position your proposal so you can **underpromise and overdeliver at all times.** Try to resist putting yourself into a corner where you can't fulfill your promises. It will be tempting in the beginning, as you will be desperate for business, but you must do what you say you can do in sales. **Intentionally position yourself better than your competitor.** Ask what their average lead time is currently. The prospect may respond with three weeks, and then you quickly say yours is two! Is it? Who cares—you say yours is just under whoever they are buying from currently and you go back and challenge your team to be able to fulfill your promise.

There is a fine line here, but know what is possible and what is impossible. If you can, always position yourself with an edge over the competition. You wouldn't say yours is four weeks if your competitor's is three weeks, would you? Even if you can't do better, at least match what your competitor is giving them to refute one less rebuttal. Your goal is to reduce any angst or rebuttal they would have for not doing business with you. I would follow it up with, "Our lead time is two weeks on average, but lately we are tracking 10.3 days from PO to shipment" (a stat I completely made up, but the more detail, the more convincing). I then later challenged my production team and executives to make my claim a reality, and they did! Thus, not a lie, but an idea that was brought to life to cater to what customers wanted and needed.

Price yourself at your most aggressive price when beginning a relationship. Capitalists won't agree, but trust me, it works. Even if you break even, keep in mind that you can build a $100-billion break-even company. You cannot build a $100-billion company losing money, remember? Use this as a compass and come back to this principle throughout your journey. Not all customers are customers you have to make money on. You can use customers to be temporary fillers in your business development, and you can use customers to get credibility. I often accepted break-even jobs to simply keep my guys busy and keep their confidence up that we were growing. You can use customers to break into new markets, and you can always grow vertically with customers after you have won them over.

When first engaging a new customer, I would go to the basement with my pricing. I would underpromise and over-deliver. I would intentionally put myself in a light that made my competitors an afterthought, but then once you win them over and you have their business, you wait. When the next product line is launched, they will be so in love with what they get from you that they won't question your pricing. Thus, then you build your business's profitability. You're nothing without customers. These are basic strategies to gain opportunity. You really should look at it as asking for opportunities and not asking for someone's business. Word it that way and they won't be as resistant. If you emphasize how hungry you are for an opportunity, people like to hear that. Hunger means you won't let them down and you will make them a priority! What you make of each opportunity and subsequent opportunities is up to you.

23

♠

Controlling Your Audience?

Your audience is anyone watching under any circumstance at all times. How do you control them?

I'm at a party. I don't know these people. I don't care to know these people, but I have an opportunity to control the atmosphere, so I do. I know the best way to deal with this is to rattle off my highlights. A guy approaches and says, "Hey, what do you do?"

If I am not vague in this situation and say, "I'm in packaging," then I reply, "I'm an entrepreneur."

He says, "Oh really, what kind?"

I respond, "Moderately successful." I have a quick tempo to my delivery when I rattle off my highlights: "I have a 75,000 sq. ft facility that produces food grade packaging. It started as a long shot, but for more than a decade, I have built one of the top three companies in the country for my respected industry."

"I'm thirty-five, and I started the company when I was twenty-four. It's been nuts! I'm humbled by the success I had when I was on my own, and now I am backed by a billion dollar PE firm and we are aiming at being $100 million in revenue in the next couple of years. I'm currently active in trying to buy other companies in our market so we can grow by acquisition and expand our national footprint." I then respond, "Hey, what do you do?"

I rattled off so many specifics and what he heard was what I call my highlights. He heard this guy is thirty-five, has a multimillion-dollar company, a 75,000 sq. ft. facility, food-grade packaging, and has been in business ten years or more, and my determination will not stop as I keep reaching higher and higher.

Again, I ask, "What do you do?"

His response: "Healthcare technology."

That's called fine-tuning your motor skills. In that situation I got myself out of small talk by overdominating the conversation. In the same way you can utilize this method to win credibility and gain business. It's all about tone, authenticity of your voice, pace, and keywords you choose when framing your highlights! Do you think this guy told anyone else at that party who or what I did? Of course he did. My story was more interesting than his, and he wanted something to small talk about. By the end of the night, people were telling me, "So I hear you're an entrepreneur?" People were coming to me elaborating on my successes and telling me my own story. Sound familiar?

If you do not realize it yet, this is how I got the entire country talking about my printing company. I let the industry come to me rather than me to the industry, remember? Word of mouth is the best way to get business and the best way to educate about your business and yourself! If you read the whole book, I have said that at least four times now! Let the industry talk about you, but let them say what you want them to say. Control what people know and how they perceive you. This is another way to do that. Do this at trade shows, do this at vendor dinners, do this when at school functions, but treat "you" as a brand of its own.

The best way to do this is to know your highlight points and what points bring you sex appeal. Be able to portray them on an audience **without** sounding like you're bragging. **Do not brag!** When you have mastered it, you won't even know you're doing it.

On the flip side, there are times you need to simply blend in. **Blending** is an attribute that is a must for an entrepreneur, a businessman, or a magician. Blending into an audience is what it sounds like. Be a chameleon; be one with your surroundings. My ability to be one with the audience allowed me to get more out of the audience in return. The more you get out of the audience, the more you will be equipped to give them what they desire.

Have you ever seen *Catch Me If You Can* with Tom Hanks and Leonardo DiCaprio? I have what Leo's character had in that movie. I have the ability to be in a room full of lawyers and fit in as if I was top of my class at Harvard Law School. I can be in a room full of doctors, and you would think I was a specialist. Blending is crucial for you to get more out of your audience. For my employees, I blended with them by never letting them see me as a guy gaining ground financially, but rather staying humble and appearing to be one with the guys. For years I drove a Honda Civic with over 200,000 miles on it to work all while having a Range Rover and Lexus in the garage at home. *I forgot to mention I sold my original Audi A4 in 2011 and spun it as a financial move to my guys at work. I explained to them business was good, but I was not making a lot of money yet, as I was pouring everything back into the company. Meanwhile I was making very good money, but doing what I could to blend and get more out of the audience.* I drove the Civic because it helped keep the guys engaged, and when I rode them harder for more effort, they never threw back in my face that I had it better than them. I did this as long as I could before it was obvious I was a huge success.

Blending gets you access to people and their real opinions. My guys would share more with me, as they saw me as just one of the guys. I took that feedback and made our culture, our company, our products better. I blended with customers or their employees by rolling my sleeves up and getting dirty alongside them on their shop floor.

Rise to the occasion and know how to dominate the room when it calls for a dominant performance. Know how to control your audience no matter who it is. But also know when to scale back and be one with the crowd. Learning to control the throttle of this skill set can be very valuable to you as a leader.

24

A Little Bit of a Lot Is a Lot

What's your goal? Everyone is different. I remember my first day of class in Entrepreneurship 101 at the University of Cincinnati when one of my teachers said that your exit strategy is just as important as your business plan. I will repeat it because it did not truly set in when I heard it, but for some reason it stuck with me. "Your exit strategy is just as important as your business plan." I guess it sounded so bizarre that I stored it away to reflect on and have always had it guiding me while building my business. Every business should have an exit strategy, but unfortunately, most are not built with one in mind. Entrepreneurs are typically consumed with launching a business or idea, but less worried about the long-term sustainability of the business.

Good entrepreneurs know how the trick ends before starting it onstage. **Remember trick #2 at the beginning of the book.** My teacher was right in so many ways I did not understand this at the time, as all I was concerned about was designing a business that was sustainable and successful. As I experienced more in business, I realized the inevitable that all things come to an end.

This is true in business as well. As an entrepreneur, do you see yourself running your company for the rest of your life? Do you see yourself handing off the day-to-day operations once the company is successful and you begin to work on your next business venture? Do you see the business being something you will pass down to future family generations to operate? How are those future generations supposed to know your vision or how to hand it off smoothly if you don't leave them a plan? Do you see yourself selling the business? If so, what is the selling point? Do you have a dollar value in mind?

When you start a business, you typically design a business plan that explains how you will execute the start of the business and how you will execute the daily operations in ideal circumstances. What if something changes in the economy, what if technology makes your product or business obsolete, and what if conditions and circumstances do not remain ideal? I guess you do need to know what your exit strategy will be and perhaps have a few endings in mind in case you need to use the trap door and get out during hard times. Remember the Mike Tyson advice? Would you be willing to cut your arm off to save your life? If the business takes a turn for the worse, do you have an exit strategy in mind? Bankruptcy? Reinvesting in capital to completely reignite your business and become competitive again?

For me, I set a pie in the sky number as my exit number, and I was vocal about my exit with my inner circle. My wife, my business partner, and those closest to me knew that when I grew a company to a certain EBITDA, I was going to sell the business. I had a vision and a strategy to secure myself as a millionaire at a young age, and if given the opportunity, I was going to cash in on it.

Now my ending changed as I matured, but the end result

was the same. In 2014 I had built the business to what I expected to in seven long years. In 2014 I went to market to sell the entire business but found a win-win scenario that allowed me to retain some ownership.

Some think I am stupid for selling when the company was on a roll with growth and profitability. People say I should have held on to all the ownership. People say I could have eventually acquired the cash I received at one time on January 27, 2015, over time with profits had I been patient. All of that may have been true, but this is my vision and my decision. I had discipline and I knew what I was trying to do. I was trying to get out of the faction I was born into. Sure, on paper I was ultra successful with assets and profitability in my company, but what if I had been in a tragic accident and incapable of working the next day? What if I got cancer? What if my wife or someone close to me got hurt? You can't pitch a perfect game forever!

Could that derail me as an entrepreneur? Sure, it could. What if the economy crashed, war broke out on US soil, etc.? No one can guarantee me that was not going to happen, and it still might. What I did was stuck with my gut and stayed disciplined. On January 27, 2015, I took a lump sum for the majority share of my company, and I was able to slide all that cash into that vault for future generations of my family to benefit from. On that day, my mission #1 to lift my family into the stadium and earn them a spot in lane 1 had been fulfilled. You tell me it was the wrong decision now. For me, it was the right one.

Furthermore, I picked the right partners to partner with, and they allowed me to retain ownership. Thus, I got to enjoy building the company to higher heights, and selling again. This was something I had not thought of doing originally, but as you mature as a professional, and as you grow, your visions and goals can audible. It's okay to audible, but have a solid plan and be disciplined in what you plan to do!

When you are an entrepreneur, you create sayings for yourself that will keep you on course and motivate you. This is not a Tony Robbins-concussed phrase to force-feed down your throat, but rather a common sense saying for myself. For me, **"A little bit of a lot is a lot"** was a quote I have asked my wife to etch on my tombstone. It means what it reads as. If there is a ton of anything, all you should aspire to have is a little bit. Be grateful for any portion you get, especially if there is a lot of it. Be willing to share and don't ever get greedy.

My favorite movie is *Willy Wonka and the Chocolate Factory* if you have not figured that out by now (the original movie with Gene Wilder). Do you remember the end of the movie when Wonka and Charlie are in the glass elevator? Wonka tells Charlie to not forget what happens to the man who suddenly gets everything he ever wanted. Charlie asks, "What happened?" And Wonka replies, "He lived happily ever after." I have this quote on my office wall, as it is a constant reminder to have a sense of peace with what I have accomplished.

Don't be greedy. Sure, I have money, but I have kids and a wife who are more valuable than any materialistic possession. I have a roof over my head and food on the table each night. I have everything I ever wanted. I need to realize this is my happily ever after. In business I never celebrate my successes, and I find it hard to unplug when at home, but you must. Thus, my saying "a little bit of a lot is a lot" is my way of keeping my feet on the ground. Whenever I am approached and shown how much more margin I can make if I cut the headcount in production or use a lesser quality material to make a finished good, I go back to my saying. My saying keeps my integrity intact and makes me realize I have enough as I have a little bit of a lot.

For me I had no coach in the printing industry. I had no understanding of what the good old boy network had as the unspoken profit margin threshold. To me, 20–30 percent sounded like a good profit. Soon after deciding on this profit margin, the question became, Why am I winning all the business I quote on? I soon realized and was educated to the fact that most printers, up until now, had always charged in excess of 60 percent profit margin. Was that a problem to me? Nope. Sounded like someone else's problem. Although 30 percent was small in comparison, it was not small if I sold a lot.

I often ask other business owners what something costs, and they respond, "What does the market bear?" I was young and naïve and perhaps I did not understand the question, so I asked them to explain. They responded, "What does the market bear?" I later learned if you're a business owner too stupid to understand how much you can fairly produce a product for, with your margin on top of what it cost you to make it, then you are one that says, "What does the market bear?" I did not know this, but I learned often that if you ask stupid business owners to think outside the box and quote you on a project outside their realm, they will respond to you with, "What does the market bear?" WTF. How about you go back to business school and learn to do costing or get your hands dirty and learn what it would take for your company to produce a good or provide a service. Why is business like this? "WHAT DOES THE MARKET BEAR!" I'll tell you what that means: it means how much can I f--- the customer before appearing to be obviously unethical? It says I'm cool with being unethical, but I don't want it to be blatant. I hate businesses like this and people who run their company like this. Why don't you just provide a fair and adequate quote, and who cares if you're 50 percent below everyone else in the world? If you can produce it for that, then do it and dominate it!

I did. I did and I blew up an old network of things that had previously worked for other print shop owners for decades. I had landed myself in the middle of an industry begging for change. My goal was to build a $100-million printing business from the beginning. At 30 percent net margin that would mean $30 million in profit per year. That would mean a company worth more than $210 million dollars! Sound good to you? When you are a twenty-five-year-old entrepreneur in an old and outdated business model with zero experience with what the industry considered the norm, it sounded great. Sure, at the time I was $800k in sales for my first year on the job, but getting to $100 million a year did not seem unrealistic. Who is so greedy that a little bit of a lot is not enough? I disrupted the market with a change in profit margin and pricing overall. I knew that meant that a lot of people in the industry were not going to like me. I wasn't there to be the most popular among my competitors, and I knew friends were far and few to come by in life. I was there to pull this company out of bankruptcy, and if I had to change the industry and the market for flexible packaging to succeed, then I would.

*Footnote about profit: Know the difference between gross and net profit. Your gross profit is how much money you make in a transaction or series of transactions, but your net profit is what your profit is after all your additional expenses and such are taken out of the profit. **Gross margin** is a company's total sales revenue minus its cost of goods sold (COGS). The **gross margin** represents the percentage of total sales revenue that the company retains after incurring the direct costs associated with producing the goods and services it sells. Direct costs are the labor, the raw material (ink, material, and adhesive), the freight, etc. The **net margin** also known as the bottom line is calculated by subtracting a company's total expenses from total revenue, thus showing what the company has earned (or lost) in a given period of time.*

So take your gross margin and now subtract the cost of the CEO and other executives/other salary paid employees. Subtract your health care expenses, maintenance and repair expenses, your rent for your place of work, legal expenses, and so much more. After all of that is subtracted from your gross margin, you get your NET BOTTOMLINE.

I have never wavered from being the Midwestern, small town, humble guy who is grateful for everything he has and more. The ability to be appreciative and show you're grateful is the game changer to achieving success.

In the middle of 2018, I sat down with an up-and-coming entrepreneur that many bet will be the next Mark Zuckerberg. I sat and listened to his goals for the software he had developed. I listened to his launch date goals, one-year goals, two-year goals, and so on. He asked for advice as a beginning entrepreneur in his midtwenties. I found the words to not lift him up or distort whether or not he could or could not achieve his goals; but rather, I found the words to ask him for a favor. The favor was for him to appreciate the journey he was about to embark on. I said to him, "Can you do me a favor?"

He replied, "Sure."

"Can you please go back to your office right now and take a ton of pictures of it for me?"

"My office?" he asked.

"Yes," I said. "In two weeks you launch software that could market disrupt a huge industry. In two weeks your life will change, and there is no telling how long it will change for. Will you be the magician of your show for a few weeks before it fails, maybe a few years before it is sold or fails due to the unforeseen, or maybe it blows up to be a massive success and like me over a decade later, you are still the magician of your business?" I asked. "Take a ton of pictures today."

Remember where you are today. My biggest regret is not

being aware that when I chose to be an entrepreneur, I chose to live out a story, and unfortunately I have no pictures to reflect on. I did not appreciate the journey, as I was so laser focused on the light at the end of the tunnel or lack thereof. I have memories of the barn, I have memories of how hard it was, but I only have one photo of the cot in my office. I wish I would have done that every year while building my company. I wish I would have been more aware and more appreciative of the journey. Had I failed, what would I have to show for it? Those bad times formed me, and I wish I could show people what I went through. Now the only way to show people is to describe it to them. Not everyone will make it, but the ability to look back on the days when you were risking it all is something you will find to be priceless years from now.

The young entrepreneur looked at me and smiled. "Great idea," he said. "I'm going to go to the office right now to take a picture of that brown couch I have been sleeping on the past six months."

I believe he got the message that I was not able to give him some magical advice to achieve success, but I could share with him some wisdom from experience and perhaps make his journey one he can remember 40 years from now. I will bet you that advice is advice he will pass down someday in the future when asked by a fellow entrepreneur.

25

Behind the Curtain

As a business owner, and as a successful millionaire, people expect you to carry yourself in a certain manner. No one really wants to get to know you as you. They want to see the white-collar guy, the polished entrepreneur, the country club personality, etc. Well, that's not me. Period. I speak my mind way too often and I am not fancy. I remember where I came from, but I want to be better than that. I get the game. You don't want to know Dru for Dru. You expect Dru to be a certain Dru, and I don't want to disappoint. Thus, the show must go on, but any magician's goal should be to gracefully get behind the curtain someday. How do you fade away?

The end goal should be to fade into the background before someone forces you out. Get behind the curtain smoothly. How do you disappear and get free from the chains? How do you get the spotlight off of you, but with finesse? When you achieve your vision, it is an out-of-body experience. It's weird. What does one do when they have achieved all their life goals? At thirty? No matter how old you are, it's surreal to achieve your dream.

When you realize you pulled off the trick, you're standing outside the tank of water, no chains, as you unlocked them all, you defined all odds, etc. What next?

This life is too short and life is too valuable to be cutthroat and to not live with a different purpose. Be there for people and be willing to share, help, listen, teach, etc. You owe it to your legacy to do more for the world that will leave a lasting impression. Spend your time grooming future generations or the next wave of professionals to do what you did. Once you can hand off the keys to the empire and the empire stands strong, you have done your job as an entrepreneur. I am in the midst of doing this now, and I am truthfully looking forward to walking away from center stage, but not for a couple more years.

I am ready to build real relationships with real friends. It will be interesting to see who my true friends are after they can't gain from my business position any longer. Will I find another for my circle of five, or is everyone in my life right now a filler? It will be interesting to show my wife who I know I truly am with the disguise of a magician turned off.

When it's time for your closing act, be a giver.

The next generation needs to know what they don't know. I owe so much to my mentors, to those guys who looked at a twenty-four-year-old kid and saw someone worth their time. Realize that you're not immortal, and if you do perhaps end up becoming an entrepreneur or if you already are an entrepreneur, you owe it to everyone to pass on the wisdom from your journey.

Whether successful or not, we can all learn from someone's story, so write a story, write a book, and give us all another set of eyes to see the world through. On October 22, 2017, my favorite mentor passed away (Kirk Kirkpatrick). It was a surreal moment, as I realize now when I have hard days, good days, have questions, need an open ear, and more, there will be no one at the end of the phone line. There will be no more words of wisdom given from him, and that is a hard thing to swallow. So much that I have become since the age of twenty-four was because of this man, and someday we will all be called to heaven.

Until then, I will reach for higher heights, try to improve the world I live in, try to lead a good and honest life, raise my children to be obedient enough to carry my flame, and build a legacy like we all should be doing.

I don't know what I will do or who will get those phone calls now, but I do know I will be at the end of someone's phone call in the future. A lot of this book was inspired by a blend of my Dmotivational moments, my hardships, my tears, my successes, and a diverse group of mentors who made me who I am. Thank you for entertaining my unique perspective on business and life.

26

♠

So You Still Want to Be an Entrepreneur?

So you still want to be an entrepreneur? Maybe you already are one, and because you're passionate about that, you were interested in learning more. Or perhaps you are ready to start a new business of your own but had a bit of fear or trepidation, as you should. The scariest time of my life was the unknown outcome while building my company. At thirty-five this is how I think, how I view the world, and how I overcame situations that most entrepreneurs will find themselves in. Business will not change, but you can now be better equipped to play the part you need play in your battle toward success.

The benefit to you as a reader is that I wrote this book for my kids.

That means you got an unfiltered and purely authentic side of me. What do you and I have in common? Where can you apply or relate to my stories? Perhaps a future encounter with a similar situation of mine will prepare you for the unknown or maybe you finish reading this book with life and business clarity.

If there are two things I want anyone to gain from reading this book, it is the importance of having a vision for your life and the understanding that the game is not over until the scoreboard clock says 0:00. It is not over because you're tired, it is not over because you failed, it is not over because no one is listening to you anymore; it is over when the clock says 0:00 or when the curtain falls! It is over when your last thread snaps and you have nothing else that holds you up. Take your vision and fine-tune it, define your vision, achieve your vision, and when you do achieve your vision, "act like you've been there before." **Remember, it's your vision, so don't act so shocked you achieved it.**

Don't let a little success change who you are and don't let people come into your life after the success who were not interested in you before the success. My stories and life experiences are not meant to lift you up and encourage you, as I am not on this journey with you. I do not know your will, your determination, or your drive. This is your act, this is your opportunity, and how you do is not up to anyone but you. Work is not meant to be fun. Success is not meant to be easy, so decide what it is you want. Mark Twain once said, "What work I have done I have done because it has been play. If it had been work I shouldn't have done it."

Mark Twain was an F'n idiot! I'm probably the only guy who would say that, but is that because I have actually done research on idiots who say work should be fun? Did you know Mark Twain (whose birth name is Samuel Clemens) was one of the all-time worst businessmen of his era! Seriously! He lost nearly $10 million dollars *before* filing bankruptcy! If the ship is sinking, file bankruptcy! Why did he wait until he bled through all of his assets? He was offered to be a part of investments, such as the "telephone," but chose to invest in publishing companies that turned upside down and said the concept of a telephone in everyone's home was ridiculous. He was so pressed for money in his old age that he had to do a public speaking tour to simply pay his living expenses until the day he died. Yeah, go ahead and listen to this guy. Do what you love and you may starve!

Work is not supposed to be fun. PERIOD! What do you want? Happiness or freedom? Unless you're freakishly gifted with a unique talent, success takes hard work! Even if you are gifted with a unique talent such as athleticism or a great singing voice, success is hard! It takes practice, practice, practice, and hard work! The word *entrepreneur* has been devalued in modern society, and everyone wants to sell you success tips and act like success comes easy. Why is there embarrassment with letting people know you struggled to become successful? If you struggled before you became successful, congrats! Way to go! Good for you for showing resilience and pushing through the hard times to climb the mountain.

(P.s. There is no such thing as free freedom. Freedom is the most expensive possession known to man. I will say there are a select few; and those are the few I wrote this book for who will ever be able to afford freedom. I want to reiterate: I am not encouraging you, nor should you be looking for me to do that. You either do or don't want it. It's about your motivation, your charisma, your ability to get others to believe, and your drive to fulfill a goal. I chose freedom for me, my family, and my future generations of family over my immediate happiness. That is being selfless and that is living life with a purpose. I sacrificed happiness for financial freedom.)

I worked really hard in my life to build a legacy, and I want everyone to find their vision, but that does not mean becoming your own boss. Accept your role in life or don't, but be more than you were born to be.

Please just be more than you were born into.

The buck stops with you.

Speaking of bucks, I should place a bet with you right now. I would bet if you and I competed in anything I would win. Period. My mental stamina is unrivaled. Don't compare yourself to me or anyone else. My physical strength is greater than anyone reading this book, I assure you. I have pushed my body to the point where most Navy Seal cadets would buckle and forfeit. Sorry, but the truth hurts. I'm not talking muscle strength but physical strength. I'm talking "waterboard me and see if I break" strength. I'm talking "being up 48 hours working on your feet running up and down a 60 ft. press line to produce a product that has to be in Sparta, Wisconsin, by 8:00 a.m. the following morning" strong. "Do what you say you're going to do" strong.

There is a true story about a project we had to produce, and due to unforeseen circumstances, we were unable to complete the job by 5:00 p.m. The job finally completed around 6:00 p.m. after pulling an all-nighter two days in a row to get it done. Now the only issue is that it needed to be 950 miles away in 14 hours.

Who does this fall on? With my body already pushed to the limit and a massive lightning storm headed right across Oklahoma, I put the skid of product in the back of a rented F250 and wrapped that pallet 50,000 times over again to keep rain from getting to the product. I strapped a tarp down over the skid and headed out to Sparta, Wisconsin, by 6:30 p.m. By 8:30 the next day, I was backing the truck up to a dock at Plant #4 of Hormel's Sparta facility. Now, going on 50 plus hours of no sleep, that is grit; that is strength beyond strength.

My eyes bloodshot, my body woozy, I unloaded that truck when I told them they would have that product. I then asked for two hours to go to a nearby hotel to get a shower, and I returned for a lunch meeting with the customer since I was there. Why waste the trip? To get face time and emphasize how important that customer was to me showed tenacity.

That customer to this day is a great customer. They are loyal, and they have never seen someone try so hard for them as I did that one time. Since then we have built a relationship where I can call them and ask if a herculean effort is needed or if next day overnight would be okay.

It would have been easy for me to lie to the customer, let them down, and take the easy way out, but I did not. This is the fabric of who I am as an individual. This is the backbone that built my company. After that lunch meeting, I hopped back into that F250 and drove 14 hours back to Texas. I could hear my heartbeat with the amount of taurine and caffeine in my body. It was a disgusting and nauseous feeling. Would you have done the same? Who else was going to do it had I not? The buck stops with the entrepreneur!

If me calling you weak or so boldly claiming I would defeat you pisses you off, that's good. That's really good. It should make you angry. Those feeling something when you read how confident I am about your defeat might be that 1 percent I'm looking for. That was the purpose of my last page and half rant.

Remember my saying: "Good things don't just happen to good people. Good people make good things happen." I believe this to be so true. I created the good in my life. I had God in my heart and within my abilities, but I chose to make the good happen. On the other side of the coin is another saying that has been around for centuries: "Sh-- happens." I believe this to be true as well. Bad things are bound to happen. It is a part of life, and it is a gift from God that he enabled us to feel both joy and sadness.

When things you fear are in your way or when bad things happen to you, you must react, overcome it, learn from it, and move on.

Fear is a natural emotion of uncertainty. Fear is a part of entrepreneurship.

Accept the fear, embrace those things you are scared of. Attack when it is attack time and hold your ground when it is time to stand strong. No vacations, no long weekends, no getaways when you are an entrepreneur. Once you commit, that's it. You're in, and you're in until you either fail or retire. Again, how many times must I repeat this? How much more can I emphasize this is not CNBC, ABC, or some major networks sugarcoated version of entreprenuership. This is real entreprenuership.

For me, as the company got bigger, my fear was not being enough. Not being good enough. Being a letdown to the guys in my shop, to the vendors that support us, etc. Unfortunately, I'm wired to take things very personal and store the pain of experiences inside my vivid imagination. For me, a bad day or a bad experience lingers on for decades, and I revert back to that pain often to help navigate my decision-making. These bad days or bad experiences add to my threads that are woven into a braided rope.

My number one reason I do everything I do is to feel appreciated. My love language is someone showing me appreciation. On the flip side of that feeling is the desire to never feel like I let people down. February 17, 2017, will forever be etched in my mind as a disgraceful day. A day I feel I let my team down. Though I was not the reason, I feel I could have done something to better prepare us for this situation. The one thing I feared for nine years had finally happened. Our largest customer left! With no warning! *Thank God I had sold majority share of the business in 2015! Had I not, I would have had to try to weather this storm on my own, but due to my decision-making, I was going to fight this fight with a billion dollars' worth of resources backing me.*

At the time our business had a concentration issue, and I was working diligently to address the issue. I spent $3.7 million in Cap Ex to buy new equipment from Italy that could run faster and give us more revenue capacity. My solution to the concentration issue was to dilute my number one customer with new business.

For those that don't know, a concentration issue in business is when you're too reliant on any one customer. It's not a good position to be in, and one you either need to make sure never happens, or if it does happen, you need to address it. A good concentration would be under 10 percent for any one customer, but in the beginnings of a business, it is natural to have concentration issues. Imagine your first customer coming on board... boom 100 percent concentration. Just be aware of it and address it. For years I battled growing my business with other clients faster than this one customer, but they continued to grow like wildfire. Finally, I went all in and brought in all new state-of-the-art equipment to address this issue. The new equipment was delivered in October 2016 and was LIVE in production by December 2016. Unfortunately, doomsday came not even 60 days after the solution was put in place.

My number one customer had gotten into an over inventory situation. Basically they had enough inventory in their Hong Kong facility to last them 11 months. Someone or several people were not doing their jobs reconciling the demand for their product to the supply in their warehouses abroad. Basically overnight, our 24/7 press shut down. Instantly twelve guys who worked that press across a 24-hour period were out of a job within our walls.

Outside our walls, this customer caused 260 jobs to be lost, as the supply chain has a trickle effect on all the companies that support them as vendors. In a millisecond 35–40 percent of my business was gone. Thus, for the first time in nine years,

I was forced to do a layoff.

How strong were my threads? Would I outlast this kind of tension? Would you, will you, or have you? We went from 49 people to 37, and it was rough. To look humans in the eye and tell them I had to part ways with them was enough to make me throw up. Oh, and I did throw up. They did nothing wrong, and yet they now had no way to provide for their families. In this moment I snapped. Like Tebow I gave a quick speech that this would never happen again, and I became a beast. In times of desperation you will choose either fight or flight; and for me I geared up for a war. Some of my other members of the leadership team fled. I went around the facility/offices and did a pulse check with those still standing.

The culture was rough, the trust level was low between myself and the workforce, and it felt exactly like I feared it would. Even though I did not cause this, I took the heat. I needed to press on. I needed to be engaged and focused. I needed a plan of attack, and I worked relentlessly to devise a plan for a comeback. **I had been punched in the mouth!** I quickly pulled my CFO into a room with a huge flat screen to rework the 2017 forecast. We dug deep into each expense account and started calling audibles and discussing budget freezes for the next three months. *How do we weather this storm?*

Though they were helpful in nurturing my emotions after February 17, living that distasteful day with me, and delivering the message to the guys on that horrible day, a few of the members on my leadership team froze after that. It was as if they expected me to carry the team back from this on my own and as if their normal effort would suffice under these circumstances. Under these circumstances, it fueled me to go get it again. Just like I did in that barn, I would go wire to wire and stir up as much activity as possible. I vowed to my team that I would rebuild, that I would build it better this time, and that never again would I allow a customer to dictate the cadence of our team. Merely eight months later, I rebuilt the company back to where it was in revenue with that one customer, but this time being split between nine new customers and over 40 new brands.

During this time of downsizing I had a company that was vulnerable, the culture was shook, and I had to be more convincing to my team inside my walls than I had to be to customers outside our facility. As a leader, you should be able to tell by instinct when you are needed as a father figure and when you are needed as a general. As you could imagine, building a company is hard enough, but it gets magnified when you are trying to get your company put back together after something like this. Despite the stress, the trips to the hospital at the age of thirty-four for high blood pressure, the mornings of anxiety attacks on the drive in to work, and more, I never showed weakness to those watching. This is what you want? This is what happened to me. I nearly died at thirty-four due to stress. Are you sure you want this? Stop looking at the glitter and understand this is so much more than what the media makes it out to be. Don't listen to these selfish motivational speakers or motivators in general. Be a realist. This is entrepreneurship. You have to constantly win your team over along with winning customers. You have to accept the losses with the wins. You have to dodge bad people intentionally trying to sabotage your efforts. If you lose, it is no one's fault but your own. AND YOU WILL LOSE!

Piece of advice: Go buy a book called *What to Do with a Problem*. It's a children's book, but buy it. Read it. It will be a vital part of your growth phase. Have your COO read it; have any person on your team read it who wants to freak out and lose their composure because they have a problem. I bought this book for my 18-month old son. I read it to him often.

This book is a part of my culture at the company and has been since the downsizing in 2017. When someone wants to complain about someone they work with, a process they don't agree with, a situation they are threatened by, or anything else, they have to read the book. After reading it, they must sign the back of the book. You will be amazed what happens once they read this book. They realize kids are being taught how to treat problems and they simply need to be reminded of how to handle it. All problems present an opportunity for change, an opportunity for progress! Life is about what you do when opportunity presents itself. Good and bad opportunities can be solved the same.

Entrepreneurship is a world of problems and puzzles.

This is the truth about entrepreneurship! So you still want to be an entrepreneur?

27

The End

I was debating how to leave those who chose to read the whole book.

Would I leave you with an open-ended ending, or would I leave you with a lame piece of advice? Would I just tell you where I was in my life and cap the story off there to be continued with my next book? Will I ever write another book? It took the passing of a good friend to get the words I needed to end this book. Keep in mind I wrote this book over an eight-year period. I chicken-scratched notes on notepads, iPads, and my computer. It wasn't until Kirk's funeral in 2017 that I had a dream that ultimately led me to my ending.

The dream was a slow-motion playback of his memorial service and a second chance to listen to those that knew him best. His pastor spoke at the memorial service, and in my dream, I re-watched his entire speech. At times the pastor cracked jokes, as he knew that was Kirk's personality, and at times he was sensitive and serious with his message. *Sarcasm was 99 percent of what came out of Kirk's mouth, and the two of us shared that character trait.* However, when the pastor quoted Kirk, there was one particular phrase that stood out. In my dream the pastor's voice got louder, the words were stronger, and I heard them slower than I had ever heard them before.

Those words were: **"Anything's worth quitting for the ones you love!"** I would not have heard these words had I not had the ability to listen.

This was a saying Kirk lived by, and the pastor left us with that quote. I immediately sat up in bed, breathing rapidly. I was excited. I remember feeling the smile on my face. I truly reached up to my face with my fingers and touched my smile. My wife was sound asleep, but I was awakened with a feeling of peace. I knew what Kirk had just given me and he wasn't even here. It was my ending to the book. This whole Dmotivation, "I'm not here to pump you up" message, and this whole "entrepreneurship is not for everyone" theme to my book, and my perfect ending came from a friend's memorial service. Think about that. I took a tragic event in my life and gained a positive from it!

I went back to sleep and woke the next morning. I called a few close friends and explained the clarity and closure I had just been given. I drove in to work on a perfectly clear day and smiled the whole drive looking up at the heavens. I said thank you to my friend up above, and when I got to the office, I wrote it down.

"Anything's worth quitting for the ones you love."

In Kirk's story, I believe this was a double-edged sword. I know he was battling temptations in his younger years, and his wife gave him an ultimatum. In this case, quitting was worth it as he loved his wife, Glenda, more than the substance.

I ask you as someone interested in being an entrepreneur,

What in your life is holding you back? What could you stop doing that is counterproductive to what you want to achieve? Is it worth quitting? As an entrepreneur, are you putting off your dream? Are you too afraid to quit your job in order to give your dreams a shot? Are you playing it safe, do you lack the confidence to pull off your magic trick, or do you lack the vision to see what God intended for your life? In order to go all in, you have to be convinced you are a 1 percenter. You have to be convinced you have the "IT" factor or that you can at least fake everyone out that you possess the "IT" factor. If you know your threads of motivation and your vision is so clear, then **don't waste another minute** in a dead-end job, **don't waste another day** talking about your dreams, and **don't be the person who wishes for things to happen**. Go create magic! Go be that entrepreneur! Go be that leader!

Isn't it worth quitting for the ones you love? Whatever you're doing today that is not helping you get closer to your utopia, stop doing it and change the course of your life! Don't waste time. No matter how much money I make, I can't buy back the minute that just passed.

On the other side of the sword, don't be fooled or falsely convinced that you have the "IT" factor when you don't. Don't get hyped up by seminars, motivational speakers, and outsiders that like to generalize the simplicity of success. Success is hard and it's not for everyone. Entrepreneurial success is the hardest, and only you know if you have the backbone to weather the storm. Only you know if you have the ability to lead, or if your natural tendencies are to follow other people's visions. In this instance, **quit dreaming and quit lying to yourself and those around you.** Don't you dare try to be an entrepreneur.

If you have a steady job, if you have your 401k, if you have a family, kids, mortgage, and responsibilities, don't you dare leverage that and put your loved ones at risk. Work hard and stay steady at the path God intended for you. Perhaps use the knowledge you gained from this book and coach your kids to take risks when the stakes aren't so high or help them identify if they could possibly be the generation to lift your family's legacy. It's better to leave your legacy at least where you started your race than to set them back. You're responsible for where you leave your heirs in this rat race. The objective is to try to elevate them just one level higher than your ancestors left you, but at the minimum don't take a step back. At minimum hold your ground and let them at least start where your ancestors allowed you to start. By being foolish and falsely motivated, you could cripple your family financially, you could hinder your children's chances at furthering their education after high school, and so much more. Quit dreaming and be who you know you are even if that means you're not a 1 percenter. **Do this for the ones you love!**

In closing, I am willing to bet you will not be a successful entrepreneur. I hate to be a Dmotivator, but that's probably the truth. I appreciate your time if you bought the book. The time is the most expensive thing you could have spent while reading this book, so I hope you take something away from this book that helps you become a better person and take action toward your dreams.

Let your show begin, and stay committed to it.

DO NOT READ BEYOND THIS POINT! You're done. The book is over. DO NOT READ BEYOND THIS POINT!

Final Words for the 1 Percenters

This part of the book is only intended for the 1 percent of people wired to accomplish greatness. What I ask is that you take what you learned from the book, apply it or don't apply it to your life, try to do something out of the ordinary, or stay in your lane, but do not read beyond this point until you have made your decision. Ideally make your decision and put this book up on a shelf for ten years. Begin your journey, and in ten years when you come back to read this, it will either be something you can relate to or not.

Basically this part of the book is not something everyone can relate to. This part of the book is really just a time for me to ask, How it's going for you? So, how is it? Is it everything you dreamed it would be? How did you handle the pressure? Is there anything you learned from the book that you applied to your journey? Did you stand on the stage and receive a standing ovation? Do you have regrets? Is there anything worth sharing with me that you think I could teach to my audience? How did you handle the day-to-day stress? Did you choose to drink or use any substances to calm your nerves? Did you gain weight? When you look at the before and after of who you were prior to your journey, do you like who you have become? Would you do it again? Did you pull off your Sleight of Hand?

What is different in your life now as far as materials? Is your heart pure, and are you a "good person"? Did you get that dream house? Where have you traveled, or what have you done that you never imagined you could have done? My life is so much different than I thought it would be. I have accomplished everything and more, but have stayed grounded. I will not settle for cheap wine anymore. I drink some of the rarest and most sought-after wine on a nightly basis. My kids have resources I could only dream of having at their age. Do yours? If not your kids, then who benefits from the success you have had? When my family travels, we go first class 90 percent of the time. Have you flown first class yet? Amazing, right?!

My kids are excelling at school, at being polite and grateful, and more. It's crazy to think I'm related to these two extremely intelligent children.

It is surreal to look over at my five-year-old and two-year-old with Beats headphones on and an iPad, flying first class around the world, but I earned that right to provide for my kids in a way most do not get to. As a family, we frequently visit New York City, Chicago, and LA in hopes to expose the kids to different cultures and experiences. When I go to these cities, I am no longer a window shopper, but I am one of those people who could actually buy nearly anything I want. It is crazy to be on Michigan Avenue in Chicago or on 5th Avenue in New York and know there are no limitations. I can clearly recall a time I was standing on both Michigan Avenue and 5th Avenue and had nothing but two sticks to rub together.

Though I do not exercise that right to buy anything I want, it is crazy to grasp the concept that I could. I recently went to New York and ran 6.2 miles through Central Park, and I am not a runner! I went to get some exercise, and my mind was continuously in awe looking out at the city through a different lens than I used to see it through. I was no longer a poser, no longer a window shopper, no longer a dreamer, and I just kept running. What would typically be a 2-mile jog turned into a 6.2-mile run. I did not even notice I was still running, and by the end I realized I did nearly the entire trail through Central Park.

My kids have been to Disney nearly every year of their life, and we plan to continue giving them these experiences. It is my philosophy that every experience when they are young helps connect different neurons in their brain and allows them to be familiar with all the world has to offer. From different climates, different smells, different visual surroundings, and more, you are a collection of your experiences. It's crazy, but who else gets to go to Maui for Christmas and New Year's? What other kid has been to Napa twice by the age of four?

As a husband, I can provide for my wife with spa treatments, nice cars, a beautiful home, a sense of security, and of course handbags! Life is not about materialistic things and I'm the last one to care about these things, but they are a nice perk to having come out the other side. A lot of people say I'm lucky and that I have it made, but what they don't realize is how hard success is to maintain once you have it. For most, they sell their company or reach success in their fifties, sixties, or older. By those statistics, you have one-third of your life left to live, preserve your wealth, and navigate this ever-changing world. For me, if God allows me to live a full life, I have two-thirds of my life to preserve the wealth, navigate this ever-changing world, survive changing economic conditions, resist temptation, and more.

All these perks can add up, and you must be smart about how you make decisions. Control your legacy the same way you controlled your business being built. Temptations are real, and you have to be disciplined. It's okay to splurge occasionally, but understand the long-term goal. I think it is stupid when people say you can't take money with you when you die. I disagree with this. I agree you cannot put it in your suit jacket and get buried with it, but you sure as hell can make a difference in your legacy. It's not about taking it with you; it's about leaving it for others. My wife and I have a trust set up, and you should as well by now. The trust instructs our loved ones how to manage the money and what to use it for after we pass away. From charities, special causes we support, my kids' inheritance, and more. Why use every penny?! I did not do this for me; did you selfishly work this hard to obtain all of this success only for you? How sad is that if you did do all of this for you? Thus, a portion of whatever you earned needs to be locked away in a vault and invested wisely so when you do die you leave a huge portion to the next generation. If you think short-term, you will spend all your resources, but if you think bigger than yourself and your family, that is how the Rockefellers and the Gates will be remembered forever. In addition to your trust, have a huge life insurance policy that is owned by the trust beneficiaries as well.

Have a budget even when resources are abundant. A budget allows you to see into the future and navigate financial milestones with clarity. I have an Excel sheet that I built that has all of my monthly expenses in it. It has all of the auto debits that will occur in a given month and all the credits that will occur in a given month. It has details around Christmas and about how much I will probably spend. It has birthdays, holidays, vacations I plan on taking, etc. Any incoming or outgoing monetary exchange is logged in this extensive Excel software. By doing this I can look out at any given moment and see how much cash will be left in my bank account 24 months ahead. If I stop working and income stops coming in, it allows me to see where I run out of immediate funds in that account. I guess I can attribute this type of budgeting habits to coming from nothing. In college, I would sit at a bar until midnight on Thursday nights because it was the night my direct deposit from work entered my bank account. If I tried to cash out my bar tab at 11:00 p.m., it would bounce my card. If I cashed out after midnight, my card would go through. I was tired of living paycheck to paycheck, so now I know how much money I have at all times, even 24 months in the future. I built the same software for my business and ran the business with that same discipline. There are times people do not cash checks right away or transactions are pending. For me I'm obsessed with knowing exactly how much liquid cash I have that is not allocated to something.

Don't get ahead of yourself and never stop visualizing where you want to go. I don't know what this life has in store for me, but I'm willing to live and embrace the next adventure. Live your life and help others live to their fullest. Lift yourself and your loved ones to new heights and never get complacent.

Wait, you didn't read this when you weren't supposed to right? This probably sounded like I was bragging, but I'm not. If you listened to me and didn't read this until you were successful, then you wouldn't see this as bragging. If you listened, you would be relating to me and not feeling angst toward me. If you are not good at listening and read it prematurely, maybe it will spark something in you that causes a desire for you to have these things as well. Either way, God bless you and good luck.

> *To live would be an awfully big adventure.*
> *To die would be an awfully big adventure.*
> —Peter Pan

They say you die twice: once when you stop breathing, and the second, a bit later on, when somebody mentions your name for the last time.

What will they say about you? How long will you live on after you pass away?

Dmotivate, LLC
Dmotivate.com